So what's all this th

This is the fourth of these c
pious maunderings and gen
this one is a bit different. Tl
theme, but I did make a vague attempt to move the
articles about a bit so there was some variety. With this, I
found I was using the blog more as a diary. Given that the
Brexit acrimony was in full flow, (it doesn't deserve the title
of a debate, as a debate presupposes people are listening
to each other) I tried to avoid it. Instead what I have done
is followed the 'lambing year.' It starts with ewes being put
to the tup in late autumn and finishes in summer with the
last of the laggards lambing and finally finishing carrying
feed to the ewes.

So because it is more of a diary, then during the long wet
spell, the rain becomes a feature. So pour yourself a really
good cup of coffee and treat yourself to a bar of chocolate.
Be brave mes enfants, together we can get through this.
Similarly later we face the beast from the east and a
drought, but all in their proper place.

Then, because it's life and even I'm not chained to the
quad but am allowed to wander at times, we have other
stuff as well. Read on and you'll meet young ladies in high
heeled cowboy boots, Sir John Moore of Corunna,
brassieres for cows, and, incidentally, David Essex.

Finally, remember that I am not a shepherd. If anything
I'm an honest cowman who has had sheep inflicted upon
him by the whims of fate. When you read on, remember
that I was merely the minion 'on the scene.' Whilst
occasionally I was forced to act as the token grown-up,
there was, sometimes in the background, sometimes in the
foreground, a proper shepherd whose sheep they were.

Soft Focus

There's no doubt about it, winter is coming in. I've caved in and lit the fire in the living room for one thing. Not only that but I find myself wearing a jumper and a jacket when I go and look sheep in the morning, even if it isn't raining. Yesterday morning was a bit special. It was bright and clear, so when you looked across the bay you could see the cloud moving slowly down the valleys on the opposite side. So it seemed a good day for a neighbour to lay cattle in for winter. Given that he was shorthanded, I gave them a hand.
Now laying cattle in can be an interesting process. If the weather is pleasant and cattle feel that there is still enough grass, then they're not particularly bothered about coming in. Similarly if it's really miserable, cold and wet, they'll just huddle under the dike and sulk, and they can be the very devil to move.
Adult cattle aren't too bad. Milk cows come in at least twice a day anyway so they get downright miffed if you forget them. But young stock can be 'interesting.' It's like escorting a bunch of lively teenagers through a busy town centre. You count them when you set off and you try to keep an eye on them, but it's only when you finally arrive and you still have the same number that you can afford to relax.
Before now I've seem perfectly sensible heifers just set off and run. There doesn't appear to be any obvious reason for this, even their mates in the same bunch look askance at them as if wondering what on earth they're playing at. Breed and character come into it. I once let a big batch of cattle into the lane. At the far end of the lane people were waiting to turn them into the yard. There was apparently fifteen minutes between the first ones arriving at the far end, and the laggards who wandered in at the end with me. First to arrive were the limis, who crashed into each other and refused to actually go into the yard until the others came but instead huddled together in a shifty manner just outside the gate.

The others made their way along the lane at a more reasonable pace, until finally I turned up with some young Belgian Blue bullocks who were ambling along like a lot of elderly milk cows without a care in the world.

There again the previous March, when we turned them out in the opposite direction, it had been somewhat different. With the scent of spring in their noses they'd thundered down the lane as if re-enacting the Pamplona Bull Run, a solid wall of cattle bursting out of the lane and into the field.

Then you get those who want to be fetched in but we've decided that it isn't time yet. One miserable day in autumn we fetched one group of cattle in. A group of dry cows saw this happen and ran down to the gate so they were convenient to bring in as well. Unfortunately it had been decided we'd leave them out another week. They had plenty of grass and were doing fine. They spent the next hour leaning over the gate looking daggers at me every time I came into sight and were still sulking next morning.

But one of the interesting things I've noticed is that, at some point in autumn, my father would always say to me, "We might as well lay cattle in. It'll be less work."

And it was true because we were no longer carrying feed round fields for them and messing about with taking them bits of hay or straw or whatever.

Then when spring came, we'd turn them back out, secure in the knowledge that they'd be far less work outside than they were inside.

So surely, following that through logically, every year should have got easier and easier until eventually there'd be almost no work at all?

Point of Comfort

Now this is almost, but not quite, real history. By that I mean it's what I remember of what my Dad told me, and that depends on how well he remembered things.

My dad was born in Askam and at the age of fourteen went into farm service because he didn't want to go into the shipyard or down the mines. He got £13 for his first half year. In 1939 he volunteered and went into the RAF. But when he reached Preston they realised he was a farm worker and therefore in a reserved occupation. So they sent him back. Until he got married and settled down he went to the hiring fairs every half year and so worked on farms from Workington down to Morecambe. Indeed he watched the bombing of Barrow from Morecambe while he was working there.

But one comment he made was about Point of Comfort at Goadsbarrow, along the coast a couple of miles from here. He remembered that during the height of the Great Depression, there used to be a lot of lads camping there. Apparently if you were unemployed and lived at home with your parents, you got a shilling a week. If you lived out, you got one shilling and sixpence. So lads would make themselves a 'tent' out of a bit of canvas and a few bits of wood and live there. On the days they had to go in to collect their money, they'd go home, give their mum the shilling and the clothes they were standing up in. They'd put on clean clothes, collect a bag of food and go back to where they were camping.

My father remembers them camping on the seaward side of the road. Now you can still see the Scar of stones, but back then he remembered there being grass on it. It might be that they also camped on open land further along, with the old road being so slow, nobody bothered to fence it.

Apparently there were a couple of other places where lads would camp. They'd play a lot of football, and with sixpence in their pocket it was even possible to think of going to the flicks on a Saturday night and getting chips on the way back.

You've been robbed!

If you produce milk there are very strict legal guidelines. One of which is that the proportion of butterfat in the milk must not fall below 3.5%. Before you throw your hands up in horror, remember an ordinary sliced loaf can be over 3.9% fat. Mind you, we bred and fed for milk quality and the milk we produced was over 4.5%. The higher level of fat means that the milk is better for butter and cheese production. Not only that, but frankly, it tastes so much better.
When I was sent to school and tried my first bottle of school milk I point blank refused to believe it was milk. It took them a week to get me to drink the disgusting stuff. Pasteurisation is as good for milk as it is for beer.
Trading Standards, Environmental Health and other bodies watch over milk. I remember one farmer being approached by Trading Standards. He had a milk round and the Trading Standards department had had complaints from some of his customers that he'd been watering his milk.
To be fair to Trading Standards, they didn't go in gung-ho, because the complaints were a bit unusual in their distribution. They came from one street. If the farmer had been watering his milk they'd have expected complaints scattered across his entire milk round. Not only that but when they took samples, there was no added water in the milk. So what they did was stay with him and watch him milk. Eventually they cracked the problem.
Cows are creatures of habit. They would come in to be milked and stand in the same place in the shippon. This meant that they were milked in the same order. Each cow's milk would be collected, poured through the cooler and then go into the bottling plant.
As this was happening, another lad was putting bottles in the crate and loading the crates onto the pickup. He loaded them in the same order, and of course did his round in the same order. What this meant was that customers often got their milk not merely from the same farm, but effectively from the same cow!

In the case of those customers who were complaining, 'their' cow was in early lactation, pushing out a lot of milk. But she was producing it with less fat and protein than she would do later in lactation. In legal terms, we have a cow who is producing whole milk which isn't legally whole milk. It was nearer to semi-skimmed.

The answer that the Trading Standards people came up with was for the farmer to introduce a holding tank in the system so the milk was more mixed. There were no more complaints.

But back then, people got their milk in glass bottles. The average milk bottle could make over 22 trips, and a broken bottle is still recyclable as glass.

Now there was one minor problem, blue tits used to break through the foil top and eat the cream.

Anyway the supermarkets stepped in. They drove the price of milk down to undercut the doorstep delivery. This they did in several ways. One way was to skim off the cream. (I know, I know, the major retailers have been metaphorically skimming off the cream for years but this time they did it for real.)

You see, in their eyes, there was a lot of wasted cream in the system. Whole milk only had to be 3.5% fat and people were getting it at 4.5% fat, and worse than that, they weren't paying anything extra for it.

But if you standardise milk down to 3.5% you've got all that extra cream which costs you nothing because you'll sell the standardised milk at the same price as real milk. Not only that but you can then sell the cream as well.

Also if you homogenise the milk so that the cream doesn't rise to the top, nobody will ever notice. After all they'll not be able to measure the missing cream if it's not visible.

Trust me, the milk tastes pathetic, but supermarkets have been able to make money out of it; especially when they didn't have to worry about bottles but just sold it in plastic containers that were somebody else's problem to dispose of or recycle.

Oh yes, and the blue tits? Well like all birds they cannot digest lactose, so milk is no good to them, but the fat at the top of the bottle was. And now with homogenised, standardised, and grossly attenuated milk, there's nothing in the bottle for them anyway.

Kids today, they show no respect.

I realise I don't count. Brought up outside town I was driving tractors at the age of eight. At the age of fifteen I just walked out of a whole class detention at 3:45pm precisely explaining that some of us had work to do. I'd promised my father I'd start milking because he needed to go to a farm sale to try and buy something. So I courteously told the teacher that if this was a problem they'd have to take it up with him. (They never did.)
But something is going wrong.
Let's get one thing straight here. It's not the kids that are going wrong. They only know the way they were brought up. So what are the parents doing wrong?
And how exactly did the grandparent generation screw up to produce the parents?

I was reading a post somebody had made on their Facebook page which, thanks to the wonder of algorithms, turned up on my wall. Effectively what had happened is that he'd gone to the Britain First (or some other such Facebook group he found nasty and unpleasant.) When you go to a new group, Facebook tell you which of your friends liked the group. He'd discovered that he'd several 'Facebook friends' who were in the group so he immediately unfriended them.
And then proceeded to brag, virtuously, about his deed.
So out of curiosity I went to the same group, and lo, it was true. There was a list of my 'Facebook friends' who'd liked the group. I looked at the list, nodded and moved on.
Then below his post I commented that, yes, I'd done the same. He immediately replied with, "Did you 'unfriend them.'

To which I replied, 'No, they're real people, I know them in the real world."

I did. They were decent young men. The sort of lads who, if they found you'd dropped your wallet, would have raced after you to hand it back. They're in work and they're hard working. Some of them are in retail, putting up with a lot of gobby crap from people of their parent's generation who'll complain about them without even raising their eyes from their phones as they do it.

These are the ones who'll be working to contribute towards my state pension should the government ever deign to pay me one. They're the ones we send to unpleasant parts of the world to die because some muppet in Westminster feels the urge to 'send out a message.' I'm not sure any more of how many friends I have with PTSD!

But anyway, just a thought; if you want people to respect you, how about being worthy of respect?

Transhumance

This is a fancy technical term for spending your life chasing after sheep, (or in extreme cases, goats.)

Actually people forget that livestock have always moved about a lot. This isn't just some modern development. If you read about Rob Roy and the 17th century Highlands, an important part of society was the Yorkshire cattle dealer who would buy this year's crop of hill cattle and have them driven south to fatten in the Vale of York.

In Cumbria we've got something similar, in that young Herdwick females (hoggs, female sheep who're not old enough to put to the tup) spend their first winter in the lowlands, whether around the perimeter of Cumbria or even further away.

Now they just get loaded into a trailer and driven there but I can remember being told that in the 1940s and 1950s my grandfather occasionally took wintering sheep from a relative who farmed up the other side of Coniston.

Back then, two men plus dogs walked the sheep south along the roads. It took them two days to walk south with the sheep, stopping the night at a farm of another relative. It's about twenty five miles and there's a limit to how fast you want to walk sheep. When they got here with the sheep, they'd spend the night here, and next day they'd walk back to Coniston again in one day. Men walk faster than sheep.

During the Foot and Mouth epidemic, there was a danger that the Herdwick breed might be wiped out by the Blair government and bureaucratic over-reaction to combating the disease. At one point it was feared that the lowland dairy farmers who were temporary custodians of the next breeding generation of the breed would just surrender them to a slaughter scheme. The thinking was that once grass started growing, the hoggs normally head back for the hills. But because of FMD movement restrictions, they couldn't. They were stuck on the dairy farm. Dairy farms need the grass for their own livestock. Whilst it's fine to have a few sheep about in winter cleaning up the remains of last year's grass, having the woolly maggots eating grass that was grown for dairy cows can be a very expensive hobby.

In reality, rather than cutting their losses and just dumping the hoggs into the government's slaughter scheme I know a lot of dairy farmers who worked with the owner of the hoggs, doing their damnedest to keep them alive and out of the claws of Defra.

Now some supermarkets are talking about not buying animals that have lived on more than one farm. They can sell it to a gullible public by calling it 'welfare.' But actually it'll drive the price of some meat down, and that will be purchased for 'manufacturing' to be sold as ready meals by the same supermarkets.

So those supermarket buyers who are trying to drive prices down for animals which have spent their lives on more than one farm are in danger of undermining traditional practices of considerable antiquity.

Still, people abusing animal welfare regulation for their own purposes is nothing new. The latest example was the fuss over animal sentience and us leaving the EU. The claim was that when we left the EU we'd have no animal welfare regulations and it was only the EU that ensured our animals didn't suffer. The hypocrisy was mind-blowing. I know people who have been attacking the EU for over a generation because it insisted we have live animal exports as part of the free movement of goods, open market etc. Suddenly they were conned by a lot of people who were looking for an excuse to attack Brexit/Wicked Tory scum (delete as the whim takes you) into claiming that the livestock shipping, bull fighting, puppy exporting EU was the only true guardian of animal welfare.

Animals in the UK have comprehensive protection under several acts. The 2006 Animal Welfare act makes it an offence to cause unnecessary suffering to any animal. 'Animal' is defined in Section 1 to include all (non-human) vertebrates and may be extended by regulation to include invertebrates on the basis of scientific evidence that "animals of the kind concerned are capable of experiencing pain or suffering". While the legislation does not specifically mention the word 'sentient', the Explanatory Notes for Section 1 mention that the Act applies to vertebrate animals as they are "currently the only demonstrably sentient animals".

There's a useful pdf that sums it up, produced by the House of Commons Library.

There again I was giving a chap a hand unloading some Swaledale hoggs onto their winter pasture. He has other jobs, and the world doesn't really think of him as a farmer. I asked him about movement licences and similar and he shrugged.

"I got a thick envelope from Defra the other day but I've not got round doing anything about it yet."

I just nodded wisely. "I see you're getting the hang of this farming business."

Never quite a passive observer

Back when I was between O levels and A levels (probably around '71 or '72) we were encouraged to borrow books out of the libraries of the various science labs at the Grammar school to read over the holiday. I borrowed two from the physics lab.

One was slim and seriously cutting edge. What had attracted my attention was the scanning electron microscope photos of various metal crystals. They were seriously fascinating and bizarre. The other was a more general textbook. I'm not sure why I picked it up but I did. When I dutifully sat down to read it there was a whole heap of boring stuff about mechanics and simple machines and suchlike. I confess to skipping them, except for the illustrations which were of a quality we'll never see the like of again. The book must have been nearly a century old.

Then I came to the section on 'The Aether'. For those of you who missed out on this stage of your education "In the late 19th century, physicists postulated that aether permeated all throughout space, providing a medium through which light could travel in a vacuum."

To be fair, it's not a bad guess, and it was only with the Michelson–Morley experiment in 1887 that they decided that as theories went, this one wasn't going to cut it. So scientists went off and invented special relativity instead. But given that even passive observation of quantum phenomena can actually change the measured result, perhaps if we reran Michelson–Morley with a different observer we'd get the aether back? At least the maths would be simpler.

OK so why exactly am I waffling on about this?

Well it just so happens that last week I was hit by one of those 24 hour bugs than laid me low for four days. My guess is that this time it was something like norovirus. I might even find out if the lab tests ever come back to tell us what virus or bacterium it was. The side effect of working with livestock is that I've had them all. I remember my late father had an attack of diahorrea and sickness and the doctor actually took a sample and sent it off to the lab. A couple of days later we got a phone call from the local environmental health department.
Official voice, "Hello I'm phoning about a salmonella outbreak."
"Oh, you'll want me Dad."
Official voice, filled with concern, "Is it possible to bring him to the phone?"
"Oh yes, but I'll have to find him first, he's out with the dog checking round young stock." Of course he was, the attack was history, he just wanted to be out an about.
Official voice……………..
Official voice, rallying gallantly, "But about the salmonella…."
"Yes, we have livestock kept under natural conditions. They eat the grass that the seagulls defecate on. "
At about that point the official voice rang off and we heard no more about it.
Mind you, whilst I say I was laid low for the last four days, I was still going out, feeding, mucking out and bedding round the few cattle that we have at the moment. It's easier than when we were milking. I can remember a number of times having a rotten night with one of these 24hr bugs, getting up at the usual time, going out to milk because it had to be done and there was nobody else to do it. It's a bad sign when you have to lie down on the floor of the milking parlour between putting the clusters on and taking the clusters off because frankly you're just too knackered to remain standing up.

As an aside, the knowledge that you'll be the one milking next morning can induce extreme moderation when somebody suggests you have a couple more drinks. My Dad used to tell of cowmen who'd had too good a Saturday night, being found during Sunday morning milking, sitting on their three legged stool, pressed against the flank of the cow, fast asleep. As somebody who did the morning milking on thirty consecutive New Year's Days, I think I've only ever seen in the New Year twice and once was by accident. (We had a cow calving.)

But anyway this morning I was looking sheep as the hail started. I did what I always do, pulled my cap on more firmly and kept going because there wasn't really any other option. I was on my way back home anyway.

Sal on the other hand was less than impressed. Have you seen those people who pull their coat collar up over their head and run for shelter? Sal somehow managed to give the impression of a Border Collie doing that. It was only my laugher echoing down the lane behind her that embarrassed her into staying with me.

It's colder now than it was when it was cold!

The temperature is rising. When I looked sheep this morning it was at least -5 centigrade and now it's probably about plus four centigrade. Yet frankly it feels far colder.

I blame the fact that whereas before everything was dry, with the thaw stuff has got wet and suddenly your hands are wet and cold.

On the positive side, the sheep seem to have been happy enough the last few days. We didn't have snow, just a very sharp frost. When I looked at Black Combe, our local hill, it was obvious that it caught a dusting of snow.

Sheep are happy enough. Dry cold combined with grass to graze and the occasional molasses bucket to have a nibble from suits them well enough. Admittedly the field this lot is on was bare enough and they were moved to somewhere with a bit more grass later that morning.

Sheep cope with the outside world pretty well, the thick fleece handles the cold nicely and if the weather is wet, well their fleece is impregnated with lanolin which keeps them dry. I've seen sheep shake themselves (in exactly the same way that a dog does) when it's raining and you can see the great shower of water fly off them.

Indeed it's when you get them inside that sheep start having problems. Put a lot of sheep into a building and they'll huddle together a bit. This will generate a lot of warmth (which is not a bad thing) but because of the water trapped on their fleeces it'll be a damp warmth. So suddenly you've got a lot of sheep who have crowded themselves together in a warm fug, and they'll start going down with pneumonia very quickly.

Cattle aren't so ostentatiously well provided for cold weather, but even they aren't too bothered. So long as they have somewhere out of the wind and plenty to eat, they'll get by. The problem with cattle is that they're bigger and heavier and in our winters, tend to leave the ground a muddy mess when it gets wet. Even then, we've had cattle do well on a large field with good dykes to keep the wind off. They had two ring feeders kept full of silage so they had plenty to eat and there was always somewhere for them to lie down out of the weather. We were going to plough that field in spring anyway.

But it doesn't look pretty. Also cattle are perfectly capable of growing a hairy coat under those conditions, so when you do fetch them home to do anything with them they can look distinctly shaggy.

One of the joys of cold weather is how quiet things get. We've seen nobody the last few days, save for two metal detectorists. They came properly prepared; not only were they dressed for the weather, but they even fetched one of those fishing shelters which they erected in the corner of the field and stacked a few flasks of hot soup and hot coffee so they could retire to it and thaw out occasionally. They came in useful when we moved the sheep. Even a metal detectorist can stand in a lane end and stop sheep going down it when you're running them along the road. Actually at the moment keeping the sheep happy and well fed is important. They should all be in the early stages of pregnancy at the moment. If a sheep's metabolism decides this is a really tough time, the system can quietly reabsorb one or more embryos to ensure that Mum makes it through the winter alive. The other issue is that grass stops growing at all when the ground temperature drops below 4 degrees Centigrade. So soon the grass will run out and I'll be back to carrying out hay and silage to them, because we're now entering one of the more important parts of lambing; which is keeping the lambs alive before they're born.

At the moment it's obvious that the sheep do have enough grass in front of them for them to feel happy about it. There are a couple of signs that they think they're running out. The first is that the older ones who remember last winter start coming up to you in spite of the presence of a dog and follow you about bleating a lot. The second sign is that sheep can start burrowing into the hedges to look for younger shoots. This presents two problems.

The first is that they can end up burrowing right through and out the other side. The second problem is that if you have a lot of briars then burrowing sheep can get themselves nicely entangled. I've even seen sheep who somehow have got themselves so entangled their feet aren't really touching the ground any more.

Under these circumstances sheep can decide that they're doomed and just give up.

So somebody has to come along and cut them out. Sal seems to have taken on her own shoulders the task of releasing trapped sheep. It's amazing how trapped sheep that have obviously been there for twenty-four hours, convincing themselves that they're stuck, see Sal hurtling towards them and 'with one bound, they're free.' Wonderful stuff, adrenalin.

Sufficient unto the day is the evil thereof

A couple of days ago I mentioned to somebody our temperature here had dropped to -7. His comment, "You should be able to get some work done with a bit of frost." Admittedly it was more pleasant checking sheep when you had the opportunity to walk across the surface of a field rather than grub about in the mud, but still, I'm not a fan of frost. We're OK with a couple of degrees but we've just too much water piping running through buildings to keep lagged; especially when cattle will happily pass a boring afternoon by chewing off the lagging.
Anyway, so much for getting some work done, one of the buildings froze. If we'd had two hundred cattle drinking they'd have kept the water running and it wouldn't have frozen, but there were only a couple of dozen. So I just made sure they had enough water for the day because the thaw was promised.
And sure enough the thaw came, and with it the burst pipe. Now a lot of our water piping is alkethane with push fit connectors or the chunky ones you can tighten by hand without faffing about with pipe-dogs. But some of it is still old fashioned galvanised. And guess which joint burst? Yes, the one where the stop tap was connected to a length of galvanised. Not only that but it was the joint at the bottom of the stop tap that split, so the stop tap was as much use as a spare bride at a wedding.

So it's a case of switching it off at the mains and because there was a water heater involved I got somebody in from our local agricultural engineers. Together we looked at the system. The galvanised pipe installed in the mid-sixties was looking rough. The problem was that we couldn't reach it without moving the water heater and that is bigger than me, fastened to the wall and both plumbed in and wired in. So we slung a pipe in to bypass it and we'll have a rethink in spring. For now the water was running again.

And somebody said, 'Now I suppose the pipe will be airlocked and you'll have all sorts of problems bleeding it through.

That's when I said "Sufficient unto the day is the evil thereof." Everybody had water 'now.' Of course this morning there were problems. I couldn't have fixed them yesterday because they hadn't happened. The problem was that there was no water going into the header tank.

Now I was pretty sure what the cause of this was. If you've ever had to work with an old fashioned ball-cock (the best sort, they're rugged, brass and last for decades) you'll know that inside them there's a valve nozzle at the end you screw into the water supply. These narrow the water supply down to a jet to work the ball-cock. However what you find is that when the water pipes freeze, all sorts of crap flakes off the inside of the pipes, and it can make its way down the pipe and block the valve nozzle.

So buggerlugs here had to fix it. The first rule of header tanks is that they're as high up as possible. If there's plenty of room above one for you to work in, the plumber's not been doing his job properly. So it's a case of tie a ladder to the beam and go up and have a look.

The second rule of header tanks is that it's always dark up there. The third rule of header tanks is that is at this point you discover your torch has finally given up the ghost.

So equipped with a rejuvenated torch, perched on the ladder, I finally got the ball-cock valve taken off (luckily there was a stop tap conveniently placed, we must have been thinking when it was put in).

I took the ball-cock into the kitchen where my fingers could warm up enough to feel anything, and I had a pair of reading glasses so I could see what was going on. To be fair to whoever put it in, there is room to work on this header tank. We used to have one where everything was so tight against the roof that when a galvanised pipe leading to the ball-cock developed a split in it, there was no way I could get in with stilsons to do anything about it. I ended up giving the pipe a coating of weld across the split to stop it leaking. Anybody who says you cannot weld galvanised pipe with water still running through it has never been desperate enough.

Anyway back to the job and ten minutes later everything is assembled and we're cooking with gas.

And an hour later I had to bleed it because part of the system had got airlocked.

Who knows, tomorrow I might have to go back and bleed another bit, but at the moment everything's got enough water.

"Therefore do not worry about tomorrow, for tomorrow will worry about itself. Each day has enough trouble of its own."

Wet!

The weather is wet! We've not seen the sun for three days and everything is just utterly grey and sodden. It's the sort of weather where cattle get pneumonia and sheep just look depressed. They see you coming and shake themselves in a pointed manner, with great clouds of water coming off their fleece.

The air is so saturated with water that it just runs down the building walls. Now is the time that really tests your electrical insulation! I remember once seeing our electrician using his test equipment on various circuits to try and find where there was a fault.

The walls were so wet because of the endless drizzle that he could touch the wall in any two places with the equipment and get a measurable current between his crocodile clips.

Just to put the tin hat on everything, we've not had proper daylight for three days either. We've been living our days in autumnal gloom. Although it's mild enough, grass has stopped growing. Personally I suspect it just cannot see the point.

It's at times like this I'm glad I don't have a lot of cattle inside. At some point you have slurry to dispose of and at the moment the ground is so waterlogged that nobody in their right mind would take a tractor onto it. It reminds me of the occasion a few years ago when I was talking to one of the contractors.

He'd been to one farm which desperately needed the slurry pit emptying and the cunning plan was to use his big tanker to blow the slurry from the lane, over the hedge into the field. No vehicles needed to go into the field, so you didn't damage the soil.

He'd blown three loads over the hedge before he noticed that water was running back onto the lane from off the field. At that point they decided on plan B. This was to blow over the opposite side of the lane because at least that way the ground sloped away from the road and if anything it would spread better.

As a technique, blowing slurry over the hedge from the road in the pouring rain tends to be frowned upon nowadays. In one case I remember the tractor driver obviously had his attention more on the road than the tanker spout, and managed to deluge one of the electrical transformers on a roadside pole. Given that a slurry tanker can quite happily put out over 500 gallons a minute, there was a bang and a quite spectacular light show. Then all the power went off.

Apparently the Electricity people were deluged by phone calls, the power had gone off just as the Jeremy Kyle show (or whatever) was about to get utterly sensational, and the people who rang in were apparently most vituperative.

Or so I was told by the three lads who came round from the Lecky board with a tank of water and a pressure hose to wash the transformer off before switching the electricity back on. They thought it was hilarious, Daytime TV washed away in a shower of slurry. To them it seemed entirely appropriate.

Sleeping in a manger?

I'm not talking about one of those twee things you see in nativity plays. I'm talking about a real manger. Years ago I was on a walking holiday in Iceland and we were well and truly in the wilds. We'd got permission to sleep in the shielings, these are the huts or bothies used by locals for when they have to accompany their animals out at pasture. As you might imagine they varied from basic to squalid. Some were merely dry-stone huts with stone and sod roofs. In some you could barely stand upright. Yet others were bigger and often incorporated corrugated iron in the structure. Some had bits where sheep had obviously been kept, but one, the largest, had a manger and hayrack. Whether they'd tied ponies or cattle there I'm not sure. Still I looked at the various places to sleep, the floor was starting to look crowded so I cleaned any rubbish out of the manger and slept in that. It was longer than I was tall and wider across than my shoulders, so there was plenty of room. With my carry-mat down first, I could crawl into my sleeping bag and be more comfortable than I had been for a while. I remember going out in the middle of the night to look at the Northern Lights. Inside the sheiling wasn't a lot warmer than outside the sheiling. The older ones with the sod roofs and thick dry-stone walls kept far warmer than those built with corrugated iron.
I can remember my father talking about various sorts of cattle housing. The traditional shippon (or byre) would have cattle tied up by the neck on a raised boose. In some places there'd be a passage in front of the cattle where you could walk up and down and feed them from.

This was known as the fothergang or foddergang. Behind the cattle was the muck channel, grape or group. I've worked with cattle in these shippons and if you had a hay loft above, they kept really snug. In the old ones without water, cattle would be allowed out to drink and then tied up again, but eventually water was piped in and each cow had a water bowl of her own. Finally cattle would be fastened to a vertical bar using a cowband running on a 'ringwiddy'.

It is surprising how many of these words are from the Norse, and interestingly I've seen the excavation reports from the Norse farms on Greenland and they built their shippons in just the same way with much the same dimensions.

My father remembered when he first started farm work before the war; in winter the shippon door would always be kept shut except when somebody was going in or out. Indeed in some farms, the finger hole in the door, which allowed you to lift the latch on the outside, even had a plug that you could stick in it to stop draughts. Nowadays everything would die of pneumonia, including the men working there, but it never seemed to be a problem back then.

In my time we moved from shippons to the cubicle house where the cow is free to walk about, get up, lie down, go to eat or drink, just as she fancies. It might or might not be better for animal welfare, who knows, but built of modern materials they're never as snug as the old shippons were. Mind you, they're a lot less work for the people looking after them. No more faffing about with a shovel and a wheelbarrow, a tractor scraper cleans them out in a tenth of the time.

I remember one Christmas Eve, we were just about finished milking on a night, which means it must have been about 6pm. Thus it would be dark. I hadn't finished with the cattle in one shippon so I'd left the light on. As I walked across the yard in the darkness, the shippon door, with a yellowish light spilling out of it, somehow seemed warm and even Christmassy.

Walking in amongst quiet cattle who'd been fed their mixed ration and were just waiting for me to throw their hay in front of them was almost restful.

There's something about working amongst cattle in those circumstances. They're dry, comfortable and full. There's the scent of their breath in the air and nobody is bullying anybody so none of them are stressed.

It's when a stirk casually scratches his head on your leg as you go to put the hay in front of him, while his mate in the same boose doesn't think your presence warrants standing up for, that you realise you're an accepted part of their world.

It's funny, to me that has always been the world of the Nativity. Forget sheep, nobody in their right mind houses sheep unless you've got blizzards coming. Yes, a donkey wouldn't be out of place, but for me it's the cattle that make it. Their casual curiosity, the warm breath, the soft questing nose with a long tongue which will tentatively wrap itself about anything that looks as if it might be edible.

Walk about cattle lying snug on Christmas Eve and you can almost hear the soft voice of a young mother soothing her child.

Betwixt and Between

I've seen a lot of comments this winter about the period between Christmas and New Year. In one newspaper a journalist was moaning about how he loses track of even what day it is and eventually the stultifying boredom of it all gets to him.

I must confess that it's never been a problem for me. With livestock, if you get two quiet days for Christmas Day and Boxing Day, you've done well. From then on you'll plunge back into normal work (with an added element of catching up) which keeps you nicely busy all the way into the New Year.

This year has been no real exception. Boxing Day and the day after were our first two fine days since about the 18th of December. Since then, as if ashamed of showing weakness, the weather has reverted to foul.

Indeed in agriculture you deal with a lot of companies who work through Christmas, although most do shut on the bank holidays (except for emergencies). On the 28th December, if I pick up the phone to a vet, an agricultural engineer, a haulier, or an auction mart, I'd expect the phone to be answered because they were working.

Even feed merchants will have some staff on to cope with emergencies. Indeed we have always had a rule, in that if you cannot get hold of a business between Christmas and New Year, do you really need them the rest of the year?

Still one of this week's jobs has been scanning sheep. People have been using ultra-sound to scan sheep to see if they're in lamb for years. I don't know whether they started doing it before the NHS did it routinely with women or not. The advantage with sheep is that not only do you have a fair idea whether the ewe is in lamb or not, you also know how many lambs she's carrying. So a ewe carrying triplets will need a lot higher plane of nutrition than one with a single.

The process is simple, the ewes move down a race and the scanner has his seat and equipment next to the race. The scanner sits alongside the ewe and runs the scanner across the ewe's tummy in front of the udder. There's very little wool there anyway so you don't need to clip it. While he does that he looks at the picture on the monitor and that tells him what's going on.

The scanner, a contractor with all his own tackle, arrives in the yard with a trailer towed by a 4x4. The trailer unpacks so you get a race along which the ewe travels, is scanned and then goes out to rejoin her mates.

As well as needing people to keep the sheep moving up the ramp and through the scanner, you also need an artist who stands there with two spray cans of marking paint.

We put a red spot on the rump if the ewe is carrying triplets. If she's barren she gets a red spot on the back of the neck. The other can has green paint in, and a green spot on the rump means she's carrying a single. Twins don't get marked up at all, they're considered the norm. Because scanning is virtually always done outside, in the cold, and probably the rain as well, the scanner will have a 'tent' of sorts to keep the worst of the weather off him and the electronics.

For the rest of us we just huddle in our waterproofs with the rain beating on us, trying to keep sheep moving. This they do sporadically.

Sometimes they will push past each other in their eagerness to follow along the race (herd animals can be like that). At other times some idiot ewe will stand in the pen with her rump blocking the entrance to the race, so nobody can get up it.

At this point you've got to stop huddling and physically turn her round so she's pointing in the right direction. At one point yesterday (as a particularly cold rain was blowing across the yard) I heard somebody say to a recalcitrant ewe, "Don't make me take my hands out of my pockets you auld witch, or you'll be sorry."

As always, checking every ewe flags up those who'll need pampering. One is due to lamb in the next two weeks. This means she managed to get herself pregnant three weeks before the tups went in. So it will be interesting to see just what sort of lambs she has. Anyway at her stage of pregnancy she needs more pampering than she'd get back out in the field. So she's now inside where we can make sure she gets a high enough quality diet. Because she's a sheep and they need company, one of the younger hoggs who isn't in lamb but looks as if it's finding winter a bit much has been kept in with it. They can keep each other company.

As we walked them back to the field after scanning, every so often a ewe would shake herself (just like a dog would) and a great sheet of water would fly off her fleece.

Happy New Year

New Year's Eve was pretty much like what you'd expect. I got two phone calls, both to discuss sheep, and we agreed that we'd get some wintering hoggs wormed for liver fluke on New Year's Day morning.

The problem is that the weather so far this winter has been remarkably wet; it's been perfect for the snails that carry the intermediate stage of the parasite.

At the moment it's so wet that when we go checking sheep in the morning, I can tell where Sal is by the splashing she makes as she runs about checking stuff.

Anyway this morning I decided to be clever. When I went out at the usual time to feed some dairy heifers, I decided I'd get the wintering hoggs handy for the gate. This is because the sheep have got two fields, and they're separated by a shallow ditch which is currently a shallow lake. I decided that if I got them from the back field to the front one, then if they stayed there, when we came to collect them an hour later they'd be so much easier to bring in.

So Sal and I went to move them. They stood looking at the water obstacle as if it were a raging torrent, and then looked at Sal, and came to the reasonable decision that, actually, the water was the least of their problems. So they scampered through it, over the crest of the hill and out of sight down to the bottom gate. Sal and I quietly left them there. We left the fields by a different gate so they couldn't see us leave. My hope was that they'd hang about round by the bottom gate, and would be wary about checking over the crest of the hill lest Sal was still there.

Then an hour later we went back to get them, a bunch of little Swaledales. And of course, they'd gone back to the far field, blithely crossing the water obstacle as if it were a matter of no concern.

Still we got them in, we got them wormed, and we took them back out again.

Indeed it didn't actually start raining until we were riding home on the quad, and it wasn't raining properly until after we'd got the quad away. So all in all, quite a civilised way to spend a New Year's Day morning.

Reminds me of a chap I knew who farmed further over, who got a phone call from a mate, just before Christmas.
"George, fancy some rough shooting?"
"Aye it'd be alright."
"Boxing Day then, we'll make a day of it, get picked up about 8am, dropped off about 9, spend a day working through the area. Then about 4pm we'll be just nicely placed for the pub so we'll go in, have a few beers, get a meal when they start serving, and we'll get picked up and fetched home about 10pm. What do you think?"
"Sounds great, but I'll be working."
"Don't worry, it's a bank holiday, nobody works."

Anyway Happy New Year to you all.

And so it begins!

When we were scanning ewes between Christmas and New Year, one ewe was ostentatiously more heavily in lamb than the others. So she was brought in and pampered a bit.
Because the weather has been so wet and disgusting, one of the hoggs that was running with the ewes was starting to look sad and bedraggled as well, so she was brought in to keep our expectant mum company.
Then the handful of fat lambs left were fetched in as well. In spite of being fed outside they were just spending more time huddled under the hedge than they were spending eating, and they gave the impression they were losing weight rather than gaining it. So they were brought in for a final week or so. So our expectant lady didn't lack for company.

Anyway, yesterday morning when I went in with the bucket to feed them, there she was, standing with her two new lambs. OK so they're born on January 7th, a month before any of the others are expected to arrive, but she'll not be the first lady to manage this sort of thing for herself without enquiring too deeply into the plans of others. Indeed she does rather give the lie to those who think that it's farmers who force sheep into early lambing. Sheep won't lamb earlier than they will lamb. We can keep the tups separate, put them out later, to ensure ewes lamb later in the season, when hopefully the weather will be better, grass will be more plentiful, and lambs cheaper to rear. The alternative is to let tups in a bit earlier, let nature take its course, and have the lambs born earlier. This means that you have to feed them more. On the other hand you might get them away at the higher prices you can see earlier in the season.

However a quick look at prices over the years will show that whilst you might hope for decent prices early in June it's very variable, and is it worth betting the farm on?

But anyway, the rest of the ladies are still out at grass, we've started giving them some concentrate feed because now they've got lambs to feed and you've got to build up both mother and her unborn lamb. But not too much. There's an art to feeding sheep at this time of year. You want ewe and lamb to be in good condition, but at the same time you don't want to have the lamb grow too big or the ewe get too fat so that you end up having a difficult birth. We've got to get the jelly-baby through the hole in the polo mint, without damaging either the jelly-baby or the polo.

And with one bound she was free! (or 'Have you got a dog who can raise the dead?')

Another day older and deeper in debt, but at least it's not raining. Indeed it's a good frost. The ground is hard, but the taps around the yard are still running. I can cope with this.

So the dog and I go to feed sheep. There's some grass that needs cleaning off from a couple of fields somebody intended to make hay on last year. They got everything they needed to make hay but the weather, so the fields never got mowed. Now, hopefully the ewes will chew the lowky old grass off for them and tidy it up a bit. Also at least the fields are relatively dry and sheep aren't paddling. But anyway, after feeding two batches of ewes, I go and take a quick look at another batch. They're not mine but we've somebody who's got health issues and various neighbours are just looking after different bits of their enterprise until they're back on their feet.

I was still on the quad, so drove into the field, and noticed one sheep had got herself stuck in some briars. I decided to check the others, make sure they were OK, before coming back to get this one untangled. Everybody was OK, and as I drove back it occurred to me that as I had a camera with me, it might not be a bad idea to get a photo of our entangled victim, just so people could see what happens.

Except Sal was on top of her game, dived over the hedge into where the sheep was, and suddenly the sheep erupted out of the tangle, running for its mates. Yep, with one bound, she was free!

Mind you that's nothing. Yesterday, I'd just got changed for church and we got a phone-call. There's a sheep stuck and probably dead in the hedge, apparently there was a crow landing on her. So I got unchanged, unleashed both quad and Sal and set off at speed. She might be alive but if she was trapped the crow would still take her eyes. Isn't Nature wonderful!

Into the field, a quick look round and spot the likely suspect. She was lying prone by the hedge. With a quad bike and a Border Collie converging on her at 30mph she leapt to her feet and was off, trailing bits of wool and briar behind her. Well if she had been dead, she wasn't now. Sal can notch up another success. She's pretty good at wandering round hedges finding trapped sheep; she seems to regard it as her particular job.

The advantages and disadvantages of ladies' high-heeled cowboy boots.

Now I've never worn cowboy boots, with or without high heels, so I approach the whole subject with a completely open mind.
Still it strikes me, that as a public service, I ought to warn people of the risks that one can run wearing these boots. I speak of course not from personal experience but instead I shall relate, in a sober and restrained manner, what happened to a lady of my acquaintance.
The daughter of a farmer, she had got a good job working for one of the organs of the state. Thus she had a salary, a civil service job contract and of course, an index linked pension coming down the line. This latter was a distant prospect when the fateful incident happened.
The particular organ of the state that the lady worked for had to deal with farmers. Thus and so it was decided they would have a stand at one of the country's leading agricultural shows. The lady of my acquaintance was an obvious person to work on the stand.
She was pleasantly cheered by the prospect, as was her father. The family were contemplating purchasing a new tractor, and daughter, being one of the people who would be using it most, was the ideal person to discuss matters with various salesmen and other company representatives. After all, daughter might have a job, but that didn't bar her from working for a living when she wasn't slouching about playing at being a civil servant. In the course of a year she probably worked more hours at home than she did at work.
So the great day came and she headed into the deep south to do her bit for her employer. But of course, all the staff on the stand were given some time off during the day to look round. She made an immediate beeline for the tractor lines.

Now then, it is a self-evident truth that any tractor salesman is happy to spend a little time talking to an attractive young lady. When that attractive young lady not merely knows what she is talking about but appears to be serious about purchasing a tractor, then your tractor salesman has been lifted direct to some higher heaven.

It has to be admitted that the tractor salesman could not have been more helpful. Not at all patronising, with no hint of sexism, he went through the complete specifications of the tractor she was interested in. Then he suggested she actually climb up into the cab and see how the layout worked for her. This she did, and liked the layout. So she started to climb out of the tractor cab.

It is at this point that her problems started. You climb down backwards, facing the tractor. This is easy enough, but not, apparently, when you're wearing ladies' high-heeled cowboy boots. Not to put too fine a point on it, she was stuck, and the salesman had to lift her down to the ground.

Now let nobody point a finger at the salesman. He was the perfect gentleman who gave the impression that lifting attractive young ladies was just another part of the job that he performed numerous times during the course of his working day.

Indeed his manner was so polite and decorous that had a patrol of the famed Saudi morality police been passing, they would doubtless have found nothing to disturb their equilibrium.

In fact the whole incident passed off in an entirely respectable manner. It's just unfortunate that one of the young lady's work colleagues happened to pass at that particular moment and captured the incident for ever on her phone.

Unwilling to be seen as less of a gentleman than the tractor salesman, I shall not reproduce the photograph.

Avoiding entanglements

Obviously it's tough being a best-selling author. After all there are only so many free lunches a chap can attend. Then with the endless free drinks, the groupies, and of course the expense account….
Sorry I was looking at the wrong list, that's what you get for being an MP. Easy mistake to make obviously.
But anyway, I have occasionally had fame tap me on the shoulder. On one occasion I was asked whether I'd like to do my own radio show on music radio. I confess I was tempted, but only briefly. I'm not somebody who can babble inanely for long periods, (Although if tempted by suitably appropriate financial recompense I could doubtless improvise.) But really, what deterred me from ever setting my foot on that road was the fact that, frankly, I just didn't like the music. I did listen to some of the output and I tried really hard to like it, but to be fair it was music destined by a cruel fate to be babbled over.
It's surprising how subjective all this stuff is. After all there was one group I used to rather sneer at as the teeny bopper boy band my little sister liked. Now, on mature reflection, I have to confess that I do think Dire Straits have produced some good stuff. Doubtless there's stuff being played now which in thirty years' time might be remembered. But still, that being said, playing endless Bon Jovi to elderly people in nursing homes does strike me as coming awfully close to being a cruel and unusual punishment.
There again, given my ability to get myself caught up in declining industries, perhaps the music industry is glad I've given them a miss. After all, they'd hardly be keen on following down the same road as Agriculture and Freelance Journalism when it comes to paying folk a living.
Still, it has to be said that there's nothing like a good dose of reality to help ground a chap and stop him getting ideas above his station. The last few days have been fine and the ground was almost starting to dry out a bit. Except that last night it rained. No, it didn't just rain, it sodding well chucked it down.

When I went out to feed sheep this morning the rain had slowed to a drizzle, but water was still streaming down both sides of the lanes. As for the fields, it had started getting silly again.

But Sal and I pressed boldly on, undeterred by the fact that when the quad stopped, I could hear the splashing of Sal's feet. Still at least the ewes were glad to see us. When you're feeding ewes the best plan is to get far enough ahead of them on the quad so that you can stop, get the feed and start putting out in little heaps on the ground before the ewes catch up with you. If you manage this then you'll probably not be trampled underfoot.

But anyway, as we check sheep, Sal always combs the hedges looking for those who've somehow got themselves entangled. With Sal bearing down on them it's amazing how they can suddenly break free. On the other hand, we do get those who're so entangled they cannot manage it. You know the bible stories about the shepherd who lost one sheep and left the ninety-nine to find it. In all probability, this is what happened to it.

When you do find a sheep this tangled up, I've found the best way to untangle it is to get hold of both back legs and just pull the sheep backwards, away from the hedge. When you think about it the sheep has been hurling itself forwards for some time and that hasn't worked.

If you pull the sheep backwards it's as if the briars have less grip. Also you can find that the briar roots have a weaker hold on the ground than the thorns have on the sheep's fleece.

Then when you've pulled the sheep free, still holding the back legs, walk it round so that it is no longer facing the hedge. Then let it go. If you let it go still facing the hedge there's every chance that the daft beggar will accelerate straight back into the briars.

There again, a mate of mine had similar problems with women. Get him untangled from one and he'd just hurl himself straight into the next.

But we left him alone with his glory.

There are days when whatever you intended, other stuff just sort of gets added to the agenda.

I had to go down to London. Virgin did their best, the train was swift and arrived on time and I drifted into London. It was expensive; my Kindle had just failed so I was forced to buy books so that I'd have something to read!

But still, it had to be done and books were bought to ensure I had something to read, at least on the train back. Anyway I checked in, dumped my gear and pondered the evening which was cold and windy. First stop was St Paul's Cathedral which is just nearby. I try and catch evensong if I can and it was there I saw it. For Christmas and Epiphany the Cathedral has a virtually life sized crib scene. It has kings, mother and child, shepherds, lambs and a border collie. All I can say is that the sculptor who created it had grasped the essential nature of the Border Collie.

There are kings, the Madonna, the Son of God, and doubtless outside in the yard there are camels, donkeys and all sorts of cattle. Our Border Collie (and it can be nothing else) ignores them all and concentrates entirely on the really important issue. The sheep.

During the service, it was announced that the Rifles were going to lay a tribute at the Memorial of Sir John Moore, Moore of Corunna. After evensong those who wanted to gathered in a side chapel and there the dean said a few words, the wreaths were laid, somebody read the poem, and six buglers played. Given that was in a side chapel, and there were, as I mentioned, six of them, I wouldn't be at all surprised if Sir John Moore heard it.

He was a decent man, a fine officer, a humanitarian and deserves to be remembered. He died at the Battle of Corunna, where his victory won time for the British army to be evacuated by sea.

The Burial of Sir John Moore after Corunna

Not a drum was heard, not a funeral note,
   As his corse to the rampart we hurried;
Not a soldier discharged his farewell shot
   O'er the grave where our hero was buried.

We buried him darkly at dead of night,
   The sods with our bayonets turning,
By the struggling moonbeam's misty light
   And the lantern dimly burning.

No useless coffin enclosed his breast,
   Not in sheet or in shroud we wound him;
But he lay like a warrior taking his rest
   With his martial cloak around him.

Few and short were the prayers we said,
   And we spoke not a word of sorrow;
But we steadfastly gazed on the face that was dead,
   And we bitterly thought of the morrow.

We thought, as we hollowed his narrow bed
   And smoothed down his lonely pillow,
That the foe and the stranger would tread o'er his head,
   And we far away on the billow!

Lightly they'll talk of the spirit that's gone,
   And o'er his cold ashes upbraid him –
But little he'll reck, if they let him sleep on
   In the grave where a Briton has laid him.

But half of our heavy task was done
   When the clock struck the hour for retiring;
And we heard the distant and random gun
   That the foe was sullenly firing.

Slowly and sadly we laid him down,
   From the field of his fame fresh and gory;
We carved not a line, and we raised not a stone,
   But we left him alone with his glory!

Charles Wolfe

Drought?

One day I will write a blog post about how hot and dry everything is, how the dust hangs in the air, and the sun beats mercilessly down on us. But today is not the day. It's still wet. In fact it's beyond that, if you'll pardon my French, it's sodding wet.
You know when a day is out to get you. I backed the quad onto the quad trailer and went to hook the trailer on. The lock that fastens over the ball hitch wasn't working. Whether it's jammed with mud or what I don't know, I made an executive decision that this wasn't a problem I was going to deal with in the pouring rain. So I put the old trailer on.
This is twice the weight and probably about twice the width. It's not a bad trailer but does have its issues.
So I put the feed in the trailer and Sal and I set off to feed the first lot of sheep. Of course I met a neighbour in the lane, and of course he was driving in the opposite direction in a reasonably wide vehicle. I pulled off the road into a gateway but of course with the old trailer on, it was still hanging out into the road. But with a bit of jiggling we managed to get past each other. So now I'm mildly wet.
In to see the first lot of ewes. This involves walking through wet sheep who're surging round you. They're coming up behind you at just the right height to hit you behind the knee. If they walk across the front of you or overtake you to the side, well they rub a sodden wet fleece all over your legs.
But everybody has their food, everybody is happy. (Except Sal, who isn't entirely happy because sheep who see food being poured out for them will run over the dog to get to it before their mates do. Sal finds this lack of respect distinctly hurtful to be honest.)
But anyway, I'm now merely wet.

Off to see the second lot. They're furthest from lambing, get a lot less feed, but perhaps because of this seem even keener to get to me before their mates do. Sal has abandoned any thought of maintaining order and is merely rolling in the coarse grass, perhaps as a way of having a bath.

Both lots of ewes are out on some land that never got mown last year because the idea was to make hay. The weather conspired to ensure that hay was never made. So the sheep are 'chewing it off.'

There is a school of thought within agriculture which says that actually you shouldn't waste time and money making hay or silage for winter, but should just leave the grass growing in the field and eat it off in situ. It's not something I've dared to do, and I've got my doubts about whether it's the sort of feed which can support new calved dairy cows. But on dryish ground with growing cattle I can see it might have a place. Still, at the moment, we're briefly and accidentally at the cutting edge of grazing management. Mind you, I suspect that like many farmers over the last five or six thousand years, we're just making the best of a bad job and putting a good face on it.

Next to look at some store lambs for a neighbour. Turn uphill and thanks to the heavy trailer frantically have to drop a gear. Sal looks on as if to ask what I'm playing at. I'm now travelling more slowly than she likes. Shrugging off the unspoken disapproval of a Border Collie we make it to the store lambs and miracles of miracles, none of them seem to have got themselves entangled in hedges, so I don't have to get wet pulling one out. Instead I just get wet driving round the perimeter to check. There again, I've been sodding wet before and I'll doubtless be sodding wet again.

Finally off to see the wintering hoggs. The age of miracles is still with us because they're all at the bottom end where I can see them all from the road. This saves me having to take the quad into the field, through a gateway which is largely underwater.

It does mean I've got to turn quad and trailer round in the lane, which isn't too bad with the smaller of the two trailers, but of course, I've got the heavier trailer to manoeuvre in the pouring rain.

Anyway, job done, everybody fed, checked and otherwise monitored. Home again, drop the trailer off, put the quad away, fasten Sal up and in for coffee. But before the coffee, everything I'm wearing is dripping wet so goes into the washing machine.

Except, strangely enough, for my socks. Normally the water runs down your jacket and trousers and pools at the bottom of your Wellingtons. I think that because I was sitting on the quad, my socks somehow stayed dry. Ah well, let's be thankful for small mercies.

Also let's be thankful for the fact actually the day wasn't too bad. On a bad day, you have to put a second lot of soaking clothes into the washing machine, and retrieve the first lot from the tumble-drier.

Fear and Greed

Feeding sheep this morning and I took some to a dozen gimmers (ewe lambs kept for breeding; these are nearly a year old). They had been chewing some grass off elsewhere but are now closer to home. I walked in with the bucket, shouted to them and rattled the bucket.

They looked up, saw the bucket and came towards me. Then they saw Sal and stopped abruptly. Sal watched them, they watched Sal. Nobody moved. The gimmers drifted forward a little. Sal continued to watch so the gimmers stopped and watched her. Then Sal shrugged and drifted off to follow a scent trail that interested her. With this the gimmers made their way towards the feed which I'd now put into their troughs.

But there were only eight of them, where had the other four got to? I could hear bleating from over the crest of the hill, and suddenly the other four appeared, saw their friends eating and hurtled towards us. Then they noticed Sal. Separated from their 'flock' they just accelerated, not wanting to be isolated away from their mates. Sal who has had to deal with this situation before made damned sure she wasn't between the sheep and their feed.

It did strike me that with her experience of the balance between greed and fear Sal ought to be producing expensive training courses for investment managers and similar. As it is I suspect that she's too wise to get caught up in the rat race. Growing ridiculously rich isn't something that seems to appeal to the Border Collie.

Anyway we went to look at the wintering hoggs. We got there and one had got its head caught in the netting. They're Swaledales so are horned sheep. Sal shot through the gate to deal with the hogg. I parked the quad and followed her. The problem is that in the presence of Sal the hogg can just keep charging forwards which achieves nothing. (Except perhaps to break the fence posts!)

Just as I was shouting, "Sit down Sal", to ensure this didn't happen, she got in front of the hogg which went backwards, unentangled itself and ran off. Sal gave me a look of dog who has absolute confidence in her abilities. She has no interest at all in selling out and training investment managers. She passed the test, she will diminish, and go into the West, and remain Sal.

Running in high heels

Not something I've ever tried to be honest. I'm tall enough as it is and my legs, decently clad in working trousers, are too utilitarian to warrant being exhibited to a dumbfounded world.
And at the moment it's not the weather for high heels. As I sit on the quad in the rain, watching the sheep fish about for the nuts I've put down for them, I can hear Sal splashing towards me. When a small Border Collie bitch splashes when walking across what is supposed to be dry ground, you know it's wet enough.
This morning the rain was coming across in great curtains. I had to slow down when driving into it because it was painful on my face if I went at any speed. Not only that but I think even Sal is losing it. She came up to jump a netting fence, totally mistimed everything jumping into the rain (or she may have slipped as she jumped) and ended up piling into the fence rather than sailing over it. She glanced at me in an embarrassed fashion to check that I hadn't seen it and then quietly jumped over it properly.
But I was on about high heels, wasn't I? It'll be about forty years ago now. It would be winter and after midnight when we were awakened by a hammering on the front door. We never use the front door to be honest, but sometimes people knock on it. Only rarely at midnight.
So my parents (whose room was above it) shouted out of the window to ask what was the problem, and I got dressed and went down to open the door. There was a barefoot young lady standing there. When my mother arrived we got her full story. Just down the lane from us was a lay-by where courting couples used to park up. She had been at a dance in Ulverston and had accepted a lift back to Barrow from somebody who had been 'more affectionate than she had intended.'
So when he stopped at the lay-by she'd seen the lights of our cubicle house. In winter when cows are housed we leave some lights on. It's easier for cows to get up for a drink or something to eat; and if they can see, they're less easily startled by anything. So they're happier.

This lass had seen the lights, opened the passenger door and had run for it. In the course of which she'd abandoned her high heels. By the time she'd worked out the lights came from outbuildings, she could see where the front door was so had hammered on that.

She was seriously nervous, so I went out to both make sure there was nobody still parked in the lay-by and to find her shoes. Whoever she'd had the lift with was gone, and I even found both her shoes. When I wandered back in she was on the phone for a taxi.

Strangely enough she'd decided that she'd get a taxi home rather than phoning for her Dad to collect her. I think she felt the taxi driver would need fewer embarrassing explanations.

Roe deer and Herdwicks, oh my.

This afternoon the weather has somehow overlooked us. So far today it has neither rained, snowed nor pelted us with hail. Given that yesterday had managed all three plus thunder and lightning, we were really expecting fog or perhaps a rain of frogs today. So mere weak sunshine seemed something of an anti-climax.

Still I took advantage of the freak weather to walk down to the bottom land and see what things were like. In theory we could be putting ewes and lambs down there in a month so it's always a good idea to check what conditions are like. It's heavy land, we rarely had cattle on after October, unless it was a particularly fine and dry back end. This year the sheep came off early in November. The result is that when I went down, whilst there was a lot of standing water, nothing was paddled. Also there was some grass. It's managed to very slowly keep growing and provided things go sensibly for the next month, it should be fit to put sheep on. We just need some dry weather for a change. Mind you, as soon as I got down there, Sal set off and three Herdwick hoggs came running up out of a beck edge where they'd been hiding.

They were nothing to do with us. I did, once, take in wintering Herdwicks. Keeping them in is like trying to wheel smoke in a barrow. They're fell sheep and whilst they might indeed be hefted to a particular bit of fell, that fell is the far side of Coniston at the moment and probably covered in snow.

Herdwicks down in the lowlands are a bit like vets at a conference somewhere. Relieved of all responsibility for being in the right place at the right time vets tend to hit the bar and Herdwicks tend to just go where they want, ignoring fences, becks, or whatever.

So the three hoggs set off with Sal following them. Close enough to keep them moving but not so close that they'd panic. I followed at a more sedate pace, getting a feel for the ground and looking for grass. Eventually I almost caught up with them and stopped. The Herdwicks had halted and were watching Sal with a degree of nervousness. Off to one side, well out of the way, were a pair of Roe deer who were watching both Sal and the Herdwicks with benign curiosity. They gave the impression that they were fans of 'One man and his dog' and were waiting for the bit where I whistled just so and Sal would put one hogg in one field whilst loading the other two into a quad trailer.

I just shouted "Send them on Sal," and she advanced on the hoggs who turned and fled across the beck to join their less adventurous flock mates. The Roe deer, doubtless disillusioned that I'd sunk so far as to use voice commands, faded seamlessly away into the hedges and rushes.

Sal trotted back to me with the look of a dog who's quite enjoyed her afternoon.

Buying hard work in

We had a bit of a tidy up, which will doubtless be followed by a 'throwing out session.' That's when we found the old hay knife. It's effectively an electric jackhammer with a blade for cutting hay or silage.
Basically back in the late 1960s we had one silage pit which was as big as we could afford, and we put as much grass in it as we could, and that way it got our dairy herd through the winter.
The problem is that we were doing 'self-feed' silage. Cows were held back from the silage face by an electric fence and just ate their way into the heap. This works great if the face isn't too high. If it's too high they burrow into the clamp and it collapses on top of them.
So we had two options, not make enough silage, or throw silage down off the top to take it down to a safe height. But silage, especially back then, was long and fibrous, and just pulling at it with a fork was damned hard work. You'd end up picking up a 'mat' at least five foot across.
Now my father had worked with hay before bailers were popular so was used to dealing with loose mowed hay. You used to cut it with a hay knife. It's a bit like a spade with a triangular blade. You can put your foot on it to get a better cut.
My father was at a farm sale somewhere and saw this electrical hay knife. He bought it at the auction and brought it home. All we had to do was use it. Well he used it during the week but at weekends I'd do the silage, and given I was about thirteen at the time, to me it was a brute of a thing and a real sod to wrestle into place. Not only that but you had to be careful where you put your feet with that blade bouncing up and down. I'm not entirely sure my mother knew what I was getting up to.
But I managed, because I'm bluidy minded and stubborn like that. Then I'd get the fork, throw what I'd cut off down onto a trailer and take it round and fork it out for heifers and others to eat.

I suppose I should have hated the blasted thing because it was big, numb and dangerous. But to me it was a sight easier than doing it the old way so was almost a great leap forward.

Now obviously we could have done down the shear grab route, although I think they came in later. Eventually we did get a tractor with a fore-end loader and a shear grab. This meant that in half an hour I could do what had taken me a fair chunk of the day. Yet this wasn't entirely without problems. Once when using the shear grab the tractor almost stalled as the grab went into the silage but fired up and the engine kept running.

Unfortunately it was running backwards. Eventually I worked out what was happening as I sat there surrounded by a cloud of diesel vapour, on a tractor which had four forward gears and twelve reverse gears!

This was, to put it bluntly, a little disconcerting, but when I stopped the tractor and started it again, the engine started up running properly. Agricultural engineers tell me that this shouldn't happen. Me, I've done it twice!

Mixed signals

I know, I know. If I start putting pictures of flowers on the blog people will be expecting Latin names and all sorts. Me, I'm a stockman, or even more precisely a cowman. So looking at flowers from a bovine perspective, they should perhaps be called, 'piquant, with a slight peppery aftertaste' or something similar.

But yes, all along the hedges the snowdrops are well out and the daffodils are heavy in bud and spring's about to burst upon us.

And the Met Office is making dire predictions along the lines that 'Winter is coming' and by this time next week travel in the UK will be impossible for anybody who cannot hitch their huskies to a dog sled.

Well it's still February and I've known March be grim before.

And of course, in theory, on the First of March the ewes should start lambing. As it is, everything is ready for them. All the pens are washed out, disinfected and bedded, straw is in place ready for further bedding round, and in theory everything is ready.

So every morning when I feed our expectant mothers I try to see if there's anybody looking particularly close to lambing. To be honest this is all a bit hit and miss. I'm the one putting feed out for them; so my view of the ewes is the front end moving towards me at speed as part of a solid phalanx of other equally peckish sheep.

Now it may be possible, if you reach a certain level of shepherding, to be able to tell how far off giving birth a ewe is by the hang of her lugs or the bags under her eyes, but between ourselves I suspect it isn't. So instead when they're eating, I circle the group once on the quad just to see if I notice anything, and then go and tour the rest of the fields they're in to make sure nobody has slunk off on her own to lamb in a snug corner somewhere.

But anyway, early next week we'll fetch the ewes in and go through them. Those who look like they'll be lambing first will stay inside then until they've lambed. (Especially if the weather does get bad.) Those who're obviously furthest from lambing will go back outside. They've got shelter, silage and feed and they'll be OK there unless we have the sort of snow this area hasn't seen since 1947.

Personally I think snow looks wonderful in photographs. But between ourselves I prefer water in a liquid state.

Making haste slowly

What you soon learn when lambing sheep is that it always starts with disaster. When you stop to think about it, this is probably inevitable, because you have a lot of sheep reaching late pregnancy together. With a dairy herd, calving tends to be far more spread out, so triumphs and disasters come at random throughout the year. But with sheep you'll often get a rush of premature or sickly lambs at the start of lambing, and then the flock largely passes through that phase (you hope) and normality is restored. But it does mean that early lambing can be more stressful and depressing than it really needs to be. As you get older and more experienced, you just come to expect it.

Now we've got most of the ladies in. They've got a bedded building to sleep in, but we put the silage in an adjacent building for them. It's open, light and will at least mean they can mooch around in the dry if it does rain. Obviously it's not desperately warm with an easterly wind blowing but they've all got their winter coats on. Also if it does get that cold they can go inside their bedded building.

Also looking across the yard and eastwards, at the moment we've no snow, so here's hoping it will stay like that.

Mind you, feeding the others who are still outside was fun. Riding into the wind on the quadbike was painful. I was glad that I got into the habit of wearing amber tinted safety glasses after my cataract surgery, because they at least keep the wind out of my eyes and I didn't have to squint. Interestingly the sheep who are still outside do seem a lot happier than they were. Whilst it might be cold, it is at least dry and a bit of cold breeze doesn't bother them in the slightest. In fact if you get out of the wind and keep in the sun it is really rather pleasant.

Certainly looking out from the top of the hill where I was feeding sheep the view was stunning. It's obvious that the Western Pennines haven't had a lot of snow yet, and the Lake District fells don't seem to have much more coverage than they had previously. Indeed Black Combe doesn't have any real snow cover at all. But with the sun shining on it all the view was well worth a bit of chill breeze.

Colder than Charity, and man, that's cold

It's been an interesting few days. Ewes have slowly started lambing, but they're hard work at the moment and even when they lamb out of the wind, it's awfully cold for a small wet lamb. Luckily today's a lot more reasonable. Mind you it's OK for some, once lambs get a bit of size; they can cope with the weather. The two oldest, those who were born on the 7th January, are perfectly happy outside when the temperature hits four below and you've more wind chill than a reasonable person ever needed. Lambs' wool is sought after for good reason.
I was chatting to a mate about the old railway men. Back in the day pretty well every village or community had its produce show and there'd be prizes for pretty well every sort of vegetable. There was even one for potatoes. You had to present three (or perhaps five) perfect potatoes all the same size etc. As a lad my Dad worked for a farmer who had four or five acres of potatoes. The men working on the railway used to drop in, dig half a row of potatoes for him, and then take away ten or a dozen perfect matching potatoes and these they'd use to make up their entries at various produce shows along the line. Apparently the farmer was at one produce show, looked at the potatoes and who had entered what and commented that this was the first time for years that his potatoes hadn't won.
It was the same when they filled the engine up with water. One would watch the water and the other would wander off picking blackberries or mushrooms.
But they were part of the rural community, as a lad my father would be sent down to the track to pick up something the driver and his mate had dropped off for the farmer.
However it's my mate's tale that tickled me most. Apparently his father had worked on the old steam trains. Carnforth was about the last depot in England to run them, so I can remember them being normal.

We went up to Ravenglass on one as part of our Sunday School trip up to the Lil Ratty. We caught a full sized steam train to take us to where we could travel on a 15 inch gauge steam train.

Anyway my mate's dad was part of a crew fetching an engine and tender back to Barrow from the north. The snow got worse until finally just outside Barrow they found a drift they couldn't get through. So they dropped out the firebox to make the engine safe and walked back. Next morning when they went with a team to clear the drift and get the engine back, they discovered there wasn't a scrap of coal left on the train.

But around the train and heading off out to the nearby housing estate there was a web of paths in the snow.

But back to sheep, we had rain today, and we've been promised more. For reasons I've never understood, there's nothing like a bit of rain to get ewes lambing. There's doubtless logic to it, but it's a logic only a sheep would be happy with.

Has Spring Sprung?

Well somebody seems to think so. At 7am yesterday morning I did my usual wander round the lambing shed to see if anything had happened. As I came out of the shed three big skeins of geese flew overhead, heading north. Obviously somebody has decided that time is pressing and the north is calling them.

On the other hand the ewes have sat there perfectly happily and have done nothing for the last twenty-four hours. It's mild and even a little damp; you'd have thought that this would have prodded them into action.

In the previous article, I mentioned a Sunday school trip, and talking to somebody later they asked if I remembered the trip we did to Manchester Opera House. Honestly after all these years I don't remember whether it was Sunday school or Mother's Union or whatever. Different labels, same community.

Thanks to the miracle that is Google I've managed to find when it was. To quote, "Mary Hopkin appeared at The Opera House Manchester 1971 in 'Cinderella' for Mills & Delfont. This pantomime starred Mary Hopkin with Arthur Askey and Lonnie Donegan. The young man playing Dandini on £55 a week was David Essex!

I confess that I remember it mainly because as a child I got to see the great Arthur Askey. There again, it appears that I saw David Essex live as well. But I wonder how many of the names anybody remembers?

Then there was the Opera House itself. We were up in the gods! Seriously on the fourth flight of stairs we left the Sherpas behind, making our own way and carrying oxygen. If we'd been any higher we'd have been sitting outside on the roof.

Somewhere down there, an apparently infinite distance away, was the stage. To be fair, it was no worse than watching it on telly because back then tellies weren't so damned big either. But then the ladies got into action and managed to get opera glasses for all the children. Back then 'your' opera glasses were clipped to the back of the seat in front of you. So they ransacked the place and found enough.

And what do I remember of the show? Not a lot to be honest. At one point they threw sweets to children in the crowd. To reach us they'd have had to use artillery. Also something happened down there because Arthur Askey dropped out of character and told part of the audience that if that happened again the show was stopping and him and the staff would have a quiet afternoon putting their feet up. And Mary Hopkin sang 'Those were the days.' A couple of years before it had been her big Number One hit.

In case you never heard it, it's at
https://www.youtube.com/watch?v=y3KEhWTnWvE

What I hadn't realised until now was that the song is far older than Mary Hopkin. It originates with a tune composed by Boris Fomin (1900–1948) with words by the poet Konstantin Podrevsky.

When you see the words of the chorus you see a refrain that has been sung by every generation.

Those were the days my friend
We thought they'd never end
We'd sing and dance forever and a day
We'd live the life we choose
We'd fight and never lose
For we were young and sure to have our way

At some point each generation must suddenly come face to face with their mortality and the knowledge that, actually, they're not special.

A big breakfast

The ewes seem to have admitted to themselves that it's lambing time and they ought to get on with it. We had three lamb last night. All the ewes are together inside the one building and they seem to be happy with that.
Cattle are different, they wander off on their own to give birth, but sheep seen perfectly happy to lamb in the middle of a huddle of other ewes. Of course this leads to the nightmare of miss-mothering where you find one ewe has pinched another ewe's lambs, whilst abandoning her own to somebody else.
I go through them last thing at night, just to check nobody is having trouble. If somebody has lambed I'll put her and her lambs in the side pens so they aren't hassled. It's interesting walking through the ewes. Some will just stand there and watch you. Some will step to one side and let you past. Some will actually push through the rest of their mates to keep away from you. Then you'll get one who wanders up to you, sniffs you and then wanders off again to find something more interesting to look at. Finally there's always one or two who you have to step over because they're sitting comfortably and see no reason to move.

We've also started to turn ewes and their young lambs outside, back onto grass. Some of them have been born well over a week, but the weather hasn't been fit for them. But now we'll have turned out over a dozen ewes and their offspring, and the lambs are rapidly finding their feet and are trying to keep up with mum. At this stage you will get sheep who struggle with big numbers, like two. So long as they've got one lamb with them, they cannot cope with the concept that there might be a second. So you've just got to keep an eye on them to make sure there isn't a lamb wandering about on its own, bleating pathetically.

First thing in the morning, I'll once more go through the lambing shed, and if anybody has lambed, I'll whisk them and their lambs into the pens at the side of the shed where nobody is going to steal their lambs and the lambs have a chance to feed. Then later I'll put feed in the troughs outside and let the ewes out of the shed so they can spend the day in the yard where they've more room to wander about. As the ewes pour out of the shed, Sal is desperately trying to squeeze past them, intent on seeing if the honest Border Collie's treat is there for her. Who needs dog treats when you can get fresh afterbirth? Or if you're a Border Collie, almost fresh afterbirth.

And that job done, it's off on the quad to check that various other sheep are OK and haven't got themselves entangled in anything. Also there's a group of tups who need a little feed to help build them up again. So I set off, and at one point glance over my shoulder, to discover Sal isn't following. I get to the top of the hill and feed the tups; Sal still hasn't appeared. So I open the gate to go in and look at the store lambs, and then I blow the horn on the quad. Now when we're moving sheep, blowing the horn on the quad tells both sheep and Sal that we are actually moving them, not just driving about checking them. So if anybody, even a neighbour, blows the horn on their quad, she immediately sets off at speed to help out! So having blown the horn on the quad I assumed I'd see Sal moving at speed towards me.

Five minutes later Sal appears. Just in time for me to drive home again! Normally she enjoys racing the quad. Not this morning she didn't, she trotted behind it wearing the expression of somebody who has eaten a far too large 'all day breakfast' only to discover that they're supposed to go for a run, when really all they want to do is sit and belch quietly somewhere.

Taking life as you find it.

There was once a shepherd who dropped his Bible while he was mending a gap in a hedge. A couple of days later, a sheep walked up to him carrying the Bible in its mouth. The old man couldn't believe his eyes. He took the precious book out of the sheep's mouth, raised his eyes heavenward and exclaimed, "It's a miracle!"
"Not really," said the sheep. "Your name is written inside the cover."

It has to be confessed that my experience of sheep is that their level of literacy is so low they struggle to read the writing on the wall.
On the other hand, it's interesting watching sheep as they go through the year. If you see them in September, they don't really want anything to do you with you. There's plenty of grass, you're a damned nuisance and the dog is a menace.
As November creeps in, the ewes start pricking up their ears as the quad approaches, and if they see you with a bag or a bucket they will follow, cautiously and speculatively.
Oh yes and the dog is still a menace.
By the time we get to Christmas, the minute you fire up the quad, every sheep within earshot starts bleating and they run after you to be first to the feed you're putting down.
The dog is no longer a menace, merely a speed bump if she gets between the ewes and the feed.

Then we have lambing. Appear in a field with a bag, bucket or quad and you will be mobbed. Sheep are at their most domesticated, you might even think that they regarded humanity as a good and useful thing.

But the dog is a menace, only now "she's a menace that will have to be dealt with firmly if she comes any closer to my lambs." Sal tends to watch from a distance when I'm feeding ewes and lambs, on the grounds that it's easier on her nerves.

Then as spring drifts into summer and feed is slowly cut back, the sheep revert to apathy and by September, you're back to being a damned nuisance again.

Lambs on the other hand don't have the memories to dwell on; they're more creatures of the immediate present. But even they slowly acquire experience. The two lambs born in early January were kept inside with their mum far longer than usual, mainly because the weather was so miserable and wet. Finally there was some reasonable weather and they and Mum were put outside.

Then we had the beast from the east nonsense. We had Siberian winds for a week and it was colder than charity. The two young lambs, with a good mum, full tummies and wearing beautiful lamb's wool onesies were happy as Larry. We had no real snow to worry about and they were just fine with sub-zero temperatures and biting winds.

Anyway now that other ewes are lambing, these two lambs and their mum have been brought back to join the others. The young lambs were put out on Sunday, because it was a nice afternoon. Monday on the other hand was miserable. In the field where the ewes and lambs are living at the moment there is a calf creep feeder. Think of it as a 'shed' with a low roof so a calf can go inside and eat cake, but mum cannot follow. One of the ewes and her lambs were sitting under the roof watching the rain. Finally the ewe decided the rain had slackened and she was hungry so she set off across the field to graze. One lamb followed her. The other waited, realised it was being abandoned, dashed out into the rain, shuddered, dashed back inside again, and stood there in an agony of indecision until it finally plucked up the courage to run out and join Mum.

At the same time, I saw one of our two January born lambs sprawled out on the grass, basking in the warmth of the rain; when you've seen the beast from the east, a bit of drizzle isn't worth bothering about.

Going home

Well the wintering Swaledales have gone home. The hoggs that were with us had to leave because in the next week the field they've been in over winter will hopefully be ploughed for potatoes. It's very much a tale of two Cumbrias at the moment.
The pickup and trailer that came to collect them had snow on it. The snow was melting and leaving pools of water under the vehicles. Here our snow is limited to an 'icing sugar effect' which disappeared by coffee time. There are times when people contact me and ask how we're doing because they've heard that villages in Cumbria are cut off. The last time that happened the village that was cut off was still in Cumbria but was ninety miles away from us and well over a thousand feet up. Here our spot height is less than a hundred feet and we've got the sea on three sides. Still one advantage of this diversity in the county is that it allows young female hill sheep to migrate downhill onto lowland farms. This has advantages for everybody. The sheep eat up the last of the previous year's grass, which means your next year's silage is better than it would be, because it's all young grass when you mow it.
From the point of view of the sheep farmer, if his hoggs stayed at home, there's not a lot of anything to feed them. So they'd have to get a lot of bought in feed which is expensive. So with wintering them away they come back bigger and fitter than they would have done if you'd tried to keep them at home, and ideally what you pay for wintering is less that what you'd pay to feed them at home. As it is, the wintered sheep don't have to get used to a new diet, they can continue just doing what they do best, which is eating grass.

So when they get home and go back out onto your grass they don't have a period of readjustment. They can just get on with eating and growing.

Back here, ewes are still lambing. They don't appear to be in any rush, and for some reason a large proportion seem to decide that late afternoon is the perfect time. They have a lot of yard to wander about on and silage feeders to graze from; they also have the lambing shed left open so they can go in there where it's warm. Some of them do. I suspect that once they've had a feed of silage they like to go somewhere snug to digest it. But do the ewes who're lambing in the afternoon go into the lambing shed where it's snug and out of the wind? Of course not, that would be too easy. So they'll lamb outside. This means that we've got to move fast before the lamb gets chilled.

At the moment we've got a mixture of singles, twins and triplets lambing. A ewe can only really feed two lambs, because they only have two teats. So ideally a ewe carrying a single lamb and a ewe carrying triplets lamb at the same time on the same day and you can pinch one of the triplets off its mum when she's not looking and give it to the mum with the single.

If they're both lambing at the same time and you've got amniotic fluid all over everything, you can often get away with it. But if the lamb being added onto the single is dry, having been born yesterday, it's a lot more hit and miss. If you're fast enough and get there with the lamb in time to soak it in amniotic fluid from its new mum, and even drape a bit of afterbirth artistically over it so she gets to lick it clean again, then you're in with a chance. This is called 'wet fostering' and you can see why. When it works it's great because it's comparatively quick and easy.

But if the ewe remains suspicious then you have to take more time over them. First stage can be just putting a halter on the ewe, with one end tied to the gate of her pen. This way she can shift about, her movement isn't restricted much, but she cannot chase the new lamb away or attack it. After a few days the new lamb will smell of her and she'll accept it anyway.

Or alternatively if the halter isn't working you have to put the ewe in the 'lamb adopter' or 'stocks'. Here she can stand up and sit down without problems. But she cannot see her lambs so she doesn't know which lamb is suckling her, so she cannot attack the 'wrong one'. This means that both lambs can feed safely and after a couple of days (or longer with particularly obdurate ewes) the lamb smells of new mum and she's happy to accept it and they can go out into the wide world and play happy families together.
Anyway back to the wintering hoggs. It's always good when fell sheep like these go home. The problem with them is that they have no real concept of hedges and fences. Herdwicks are the worst, they just escape. We were lucky these little Swaledales didn't actually get out on us. I did have to nip in three or four times to fix gaps in the wire they'd found, but that was the limit to it. We wintered Herdwicks one year. Before Christmas they were fine. We had no problems. After New Year I don't think any of them bothered staying in the correct field for a whole afternoon! As I said, we only wintered Herdwicks once.

Little one at large

When you go into a lambing shed first thing in the morning you never really know what you're going to find. On some mornings I've made my way from one end of the shed to the other and back, to discover absolutely nothing has happened. On other occasions you'll find that the adoring mum and adorable offspring are the first thing you see as you open the door.
This morning was a fine example of just what you can find. From the door I could see that at least one had lambed. She was a mule ewe who'd had triplets. One had been born dead but the other two were both up on their feet and looked well. So I picked up the lambs and walked backwards towards the individual pens. She is a good mother, she followed me closely and when I put the lambs in the pen she followed without hesitation.

I shut the gate, now she wasn't going to have anybody hassling her, trying to steal her lambs.

By this time I'd noticed there was another ewe had lambed so I went up to collect her. She had two, but frankly they weren't really a set. Still she had been scanned to have twins so I collected her lambs and led her to a pen.

By this time I'd heard bleating from further up the shed. So I went back to the far end and there was a black faced Suffolk ewe with a single lamb. There was an issue here in that the lamb she had looked awfully like one of the lambs the second ewe had. It did look as if the two ewes had managed to swap lambs somewhere along the line.

Anyway the Suffolk wouldn't follow her lamb, so I put the lamb in the pen and manoeuvred the ewe until finally it saw the lamb and went into the pen to join it. I looked round, found nothing else, and so I dipped the navels of the five lambs with iodine (to stop infection getting in) and gave them a squirt of 'Scour Halt' into their mouths. This protects them from bacterial neonatal disease, sometimes known as 'watery mouth.' Basically at that age they're programmed to suck anything. So when they go under the ewe to suckle, firstly her teats aren't as clean as they might be, and anyway the lamb might try sucking on a piece of wool. So this procedure saves a lot of little lives.

Anyway a couple of hours later I would feed the ewes who hadn't lambed. This involves putting feed into troughs into the yard and then letting the ewes out of the lambing shed. When you do this you have to keep well out of the road or they'll tread you underfoot.

But as I was filling my bucket with feed to put in the troughs it was obvious that I could hear a lamb bleating from the lambing shed. Not only that, but the bleating was coming from the opposite end of the shed to the individual pens holding the ewes and lambs. So had somebody else lambed?

Anyway I decided that before I opened the gate to let the ewes out I'd walk through the ewes just to check what was happening. Otherwise the ewe who'd just lambed could be carried out in the stampede and her lamb might even get trodden underfoot.

Eventually I found where the bleating was coming from. A new born lamb had managed to creep behind the water trough and of course now it was cold and hungry and wanted Mum.

So I rescued the lamb and gave it to the black faced Suffolk who only had one lamb and who had lambed in that general area. She seemed perfectly happy to see it. But now we have two ewes who seem to have produced four lambs between them and then each picked the two they liked best without worrying about whose they actually were. Still if they're happy then they can keep them.

Of course our wandering friend did look a bit chilled so he's in the warming box.

This is a cut-off plastic silage additive drum (well washed out and it's done this job for a number of years.) There's a picture of it on the front cover. It features an ordinary light bulb shining down to provide warmth. Also you'll see there's a fan heater there as well in case you need more heat. The metal thing to the left with a white plastic jacket is an old milk pump motor which is still there from when we milked back in the 1990s. As you can see the young fellow is up on his feet and seems none the worse for his adventures.

Wonderful stuff, genetics.

So it was about 8pm last night and I decided it was time to walk through the lambing ewes and see if anybody was up to anything. I arrived to find a black faced Suffolk ewe with four new born lambs. Two were black and two were white. There was a problem with this, she hadn't actually lambed, she'd just borrowed them.

A walk through the rest of the ewes produced a Leicester (they're the ones with the Roman nose) who had lambed and was quietly ignoring everything that was going on. So I put the Leicester in one of the individual pens and tried to work out what on earth had been going on. She had been scanned for triplets, so was she about to produce a third? Certainly she didn't want any of the four I could offer her.

Anyway I walked slowly and methodically through the rest of the ewes, nobody else had lambed. Therefore all four were hers. I was about convinced but she most certainly wasn't. I tried her with the two black ones, whilst the Suffolk insisted on clutching the other pair to her bosom muttering 'my precioussessss.'

Eventually we haltered the Leicester to stop her driving the lambs off and put all four in with her and left her to get on with it. She seems to have accepted them. At some point we'll borrow two to put on ewes who only have a single lamb because there's no way she'll be able to feed them all.

But whilst I was looking round, I spotted a little Shearling who was starting to lamb. A shearling is a sheep who has been sheared once. As they're never sheared in their first year when they're lambs, it means she's approaching two years old. She has a twin brother out there who is being kept as a tup. He is probably half as long again as her and taller. She was small but was certainly big enough to tup, because at this point we were expecting her to produce some sort of growth spurt (like her brother has done). She's obviously cut from a very different set of genes to her brother as she has remained determinedly small, so when it came to her lambing we were expecting issues. One quick check inside her convinced a far more experienced shepherd than me that there was no way the lamb was coming out the usual way. So at ten to ten last night we phoned the vet to tell him the shearling was on her way. We lifted her into the back of the car and she went off for a caesarean. Just part of the ordinary working day for a large animal vet.

Mum

One thing you realise during lambing is that not all mothers are created equal. With sheep you get all sorts. For an animal that was supposedly bred to enhance the maternal instinct, it might be time to up the stakes and see if a spot of genetic modification might not speed the job.
Breed seems to have something to do with the maternal instinct. The fell breeds seem to have it in spades. So most breeding sheep are a crossbreed, often with a fell sheep as their mother, and a lowland breed as a father. This means that the offspring should get size and milkiness from the father and toughness and the maternal instinct from the mother. This in theory produces the best of both worlds, and this crossbreed is normally known as 'The Mule.'
The trouble is that this sort of breeding programme demands that most sheep farmers buy in all their replacements, as few have land suitable for fell sheep. So farmers will have to buy in their Mules. A lot of farmers will buy in some Mules, but will also keep a few useful looking ewe lambs from last year's crop. So the lowland side of the breeding starts to take over, and perhaps they're not as strongly maternal as their mothers. But to be fair to them, they can be more docile and produce bigger lambs who grow faster.
Note, these are very general traits and individual ewes will vary widely. But across a thousand ewes and several generations the traits can become more noticeable.
One example is what happens when the dog appears. Most ewes will stamp a front foot at it, and perhaps even make a token charge it if it comes too near. This is just to let the dog know that there are rules and limits. A big Swaledale ewe (a fell breed with a fine set of horns) will just stand there and stare the dog out. "Come on dog if you think you're hard enough." Most dogs with any sheep experience will remember a previous appointment at this point and slink quietly off. They know they're dealing with a ewe who will charge, and will happily convert the charge into a hot pursuit!

So at one extreme you have the sheep who are really good mums. The Leicester who had quads, which she produced without assistance, is an exemplar. Once she'd got over the initial shock, she took to them, licked them down, made sure they were fed and didn't sit on them. We took one of her lambs to put on another ewe who'd lost hers, and the Leicester is still feeding three and feeding them well.

The good mums are a pleasure to work with. When they've lambed they're easy to move. You pick up the lambs and the ewe follows behind you, her nose never more than six inches from her lambs.

You can get those who can be 'over maternal.' This is the ewe who is so keen on having lambs she steals them from other sheep even when she hasn't lambed herself. These can be a real pain in the proverbial. A ewe has just lambed and you're trying to quietly manoeuvre her into a separate pen so she can lick them down, feed them and bond with them away from the hurly burly. As you do this some idiot keeps charging in and tries to push the other ewe out! She is often the target of harsh language and even uncharitable comments. Still, to be fair, when she finally does get round to lambing she can normally be trusted to be a good mum, and with lambs of her own she doesn't seem to feel the urge to steal more.

Then you get those who are just thick. You pick up the lambs and walk backwards so that she can always see them. They're bleating at her. She follows a few reluctant steps and then decides it's a con and runs back to wherever it was she lambed. So you go back with the lambs, put them in front of her, and she discovers them. All is sweetness and light. You pick them up because she's lambed in the middle of the yard in the pouring rain and the lambs need to be inside. The minute you pick them up, they become invisible and she charges off somewhere to try and find them. Last year I had one ewe like this who lambed outside. This means lifting the lambs into the quad trailer. The ewe follows them in and I shut the trailer gate behind her and fetch her home rejoicing.

In the case of one bluidy auld witch, I finally had to fetch the lambs home and put them under the heat lamp. Then I went back, fetched in all sixty ewes as it was the only way I'd get the new lambed ewe inside. Once they were in the lambing shed I could finally catch Mum and stick her in a single pen. Then I let the others back out and brought the erring mum her lambs back. She took to them immediately but frankly it had taken nearly an hour to do a job that should take ten minutes at the most.

Then you have hoggs and shearlings. Hoggs are about a year old when they have their first lamb, shearlings are about two years old. (They've been sheared, hence the name.) You're always careful about putting hoggs in with the tup. You want to make sure the hogg is big enough. Obviously in nature, nobody is that careful. Anything female that comes in season will get tupped. So in a wild situation you'll lose a lot of young females who're too small to lamb.

The problem with these young sheep is that they have the instincts but it's as if they've never been activated. So they fire up in a most haphazard manner. This morning I checked the lambing shed at 5:30am, nothing was happening. At 7am when we went in, one hogg had produced twin lambs, licked them down and was feeding them. A couple of hours later she was happy enough to follow them out of the lambing shed across to the pens where we'd let her stay and bond with them for a few days. Yet I've seen hoggs that lambed, took one look at what they'd produced and just abandoned it. If you get the young ewe and lamb into a small pen where Mum cannot avoid the lamb, they'll normally get over their initial panic and their instincts will kick in.

Still lambing hoggs is a somewhat uncertain process. To them everything is new and at times quite interesting. So don't be surprised to find the young mum climbing half way up her pen gate, just to get a better view of what's going on.

Stick to what you know best?

In my case this appears to be mud! We've had a wet winter, but the 'Beast from the east' and the constant, biting easterly winds did one good thing. They dried the ground up. It became possible to travel and sheep could wander about pretty well everywhere without leaving a mess.
Then we had the endless rain of the past few days. It has chucked it down. I've seen water running across roads in places I've never seen it run before. So a couple of days ago I had let sheep across the beck into another, drier field.
This sort of worked; the ewes ignored the driving rain and poured across the bridge after me. Some of the lambs followed, but the rest sat in what shelter they could find and just glared at me. Indeed they just glared at Sal as well as she tried to mooch among them and just get them moving a bit. Finally we left them on the grounds that their mums would come back to them later. In fact when the rain stopped and the sun came out a bit, they did condescend to join the rest of the flock.
Sal isn't really enjoying it at the moment, the lambs have got to the stage where they'll just run and play in bunches. So she wandered about the field well out of everybody's way so the ewes weren't feeling threatened. Then suddenly thirty lambs descended upon her and started frolicking around her. Now that as such isn't the problem. They're not going to attack her, she isn't going to attack them, and if they get to be a nuisance she'll go off or wait for them to just run off at random to play with something else.
The problem is when Mum notices what's going on and thunders across to deal with this wicked wolf descendent who is leading her poor darlings astray. There are times a dutiful dog cannot do right for doing wrong!
 So Sal knows that you do not stand between mother and offspring. She's not stupid, it's the first rule.

So what exactly do you do when the lamb decides to play hide and seek with Mum and uses you as something to hide behind? At this point Sal merely makes her excuses and leaves at speed to avoid trouble.

A bad day?

Sal is less than happy. Normally when I go out on the quad she runs behind me (because the lanes are narrow) or even tries to outrun me when we're in a field.
But at the moment we've got a lot of ewes outside with youngish lambs. The lambs have got to the adventurous stage. When I feed their mothers this means the ewes gather together, running in from all over the field. The lambs obviously run with them. But they meet up with a lot of other running lambs and of course, they just keep on running together. I suspect the technical term is gambolling. It does have a certain charm.
From my point of view it isn't actually a problem. Yes I've got to make sure none are gambolling around the quad or trailer, because they tend to change course pretty much at random. The other thing that can happen is that they decide to race the quad. I've known people who've driven out of the gate into the lane, suddenly to discover that they're surrounded by a sea of lambs who proceed to split up and run in different directions. So you have to make sure that by the time you need to leave the field the lambs are interested in something else. To be fair this isn't too difficult, a lamb doesn't have all that long an attention span. Give them a couple of minutes then they'll head back to Mum. Provided they can see her!
But from Sal's point of view, she wanders into the field and swings wide to keep out of everybody's way. Unfortunately on this occasion her wise actions brought her too close to an elderly ewe who wasn't going to stand for any canine nonsense. Sal managed to dodge her, but still she wasn't happy about it.

The other thing we had was lambs in the 'wrong bit'. When you're the size of a lamb, fences are something larger people worry about. So we have two lots of ewes and their lambs in two paddocks, separated by a wire netting fence. Two lambs got through the fence somehow. They seem to use a form of Brownian motion, just moving about and suddenly being on the wrong side. The fact that they were on the wrong side of the fence was brought to my attention by their pathetic bleating. Mum was bleating back, but she couldn't get to them because of the fence, and of course now they needed to get back, the lambs found the fence to be an impassable obstacle.

By now it was 10pm, black as the ace of spades and a cold rain was starting to fall. Something had to be done now, because lambs of this age can suffer badly if they go hungry, cold and wet, overnight.

So we opened the gate between the two paddocks. The problem is this is being done by torch light. Mum cleared off when the torches started shining in her direction. The lambs were confused because some places were light and some weren't. Obviously they didn't stick together. There are probably excellent evolutionary reasons for running off in different directions, but under the circumstances I do wish there was an override code we could input.

Anyway, by accident, the lambs went through the gate and I shut it after them. We switched the torches off and Mum, reassured by the absence of ostentatious witchcraft, came back to join her little darlings.

But anyway that was the day before yesterday. Today was so warm I was walking out in shirt sleeves. Is spring about to happen? It's not been a bad day.

Spring has sprung?

It's been longer than normal since I last posted. To be honest I've been busy. Yes, Jim has been working for a living. It's something I'm supposed to do from time to time. But anyway, at the start of the week I had to go down to London for agricultural meetings. They were interesting. Agriculture is in a very unusual position at the moment. Defra is consulting and because two years ago nobody expected us to be where we are, nobody has 'a plan.'
This is a good thing; it means the consultation is real. The cynic in me normally reckons that you read a standard Defra consultation document, as produced under all governments (party makes no difference here) and you'll find three options.

One is too hot,
One is too cold,
And one is just right.

And it's obviously the Goldilocks option that they want to implement and you are supposed to agree with.
But this time it's obvious that Defra is listening and happy to seek guidance. Which is surely a good thing?
But when I was down in London, the world changed. Obviously London is always too hot and unpleasant, but it was merely a taste of things to come. When I arrived home, Spring had finally arrived. No ethereal maiden elegantly reclining amidst the early flowers. No this year we got the harassed young mum, frantically juggling far too many things at once, who passed through at speed, smelling vaguely of nappies.
But still it was good to see her and everybody is enjoying it. Previously, Sal had abandoned running behind the quad when I went to feed ewes and lambs. Mainly because she had had a bellyful of the general unpleasantness. Now she comes with me again.

Whereas previously ewes glowered at the lamb eating wolf descendent that was threatening to prey on their darlings, now they smile beneficently at her as she stalwartly patrols the fringes of the flock guarding them from some untold peril. She's still doing exactly what she had been doing, but even the sheep seem to have decided that spring is in the air and the world is suddenly a better, indeed a more wonderful, place.

Not only that but somebody borrowed a loadall and we're spring cleaning with a vengeance. Plastic in that skip for recycling, metal in that skip for sale. I've spent the day cutting up the scrap wood that has emerged out of the various heaps, getting ready for winter.

I've been busy in other things as well. I launched a new collection of stories, and obviously I had to tell people so they knew it was available for purchase. (This is a courteous way of saying I did my best to make the internet hideous for people with constant adverts screaming 'buy my book.')

One way I do this is produce stories for other people's blogs. They tend to be people who like the tales of Tallis Steelyard, and so they're pleased to host a story.

I'll do a number of stories, and try and link them to a theme. This means that people can follow the story from blog to blog, getting to see a lot of interesting blogs in passing. Effectively it links them together as a 'tour'. Even more importantly people get to see my stories, like them and invest 99p in a collection of them!

This time, I took my inspiration for the promotion from Mussorgsky - Pictures at an Exhibition. I kept the vague theme of Mussorgsky's pictures but found some of my own and had Tallis Steelyard write a story for each picture. For other people's blogs this works well, the internet needs pictures and I'm using the highest quality of art.

Half way through the tour I realised just how much work I'd done on these stories. They were virtually a novella on their own! So I collected together all these stories, and put them together into an ebook. So what you get is thirteen stories plus the pictures that inspired them.

Go on, treat yourself, what else can you get for 99p

https://www.amazon.co.uk/Tallis-Steelyard-Pictures-Exhibition-illustrated-ebook/dp/B07C5V726Y

As one reviewer commented, "An assortment of Tallis Steelyard tales to make the reader chuckle, laugh, wipe away a sad tear, and all emotions in between.
Every story is a stand-alone gem."

Lambing almost live

Well we've about made it. There are definitely two left to lamb but they could take a fortnight to make their minds up. Then there are three hoggs who might possibly be in lamb but again they could be even further off.
So the curtain may not have come down on the show, but in reality, we've moved on.
I think three brief sketches will sum up where we are. The blackthorn is in flower, and this morning as I was feeding one group of ewes and lambs I caught the scent of gorse. It hung heavy in the air by the hedge. Grass is definitely growing faster than it's being eaten, the ground is drier than it was last week and whilst Sal might find herself being harassed by frolicking lambs, the ewes by and large seem to ignore her as a threat. I think they have the feeling that, if Sal is a threat, the lambs can now run faster than the ewes can, so they're big enough to cope on their own.
We're moving onto a new season's problems. One ewe was looking a bit dopey in a field. (Even by the undemanding standards of sheep she didn't look bright.) The problem with herd animals generally is that they make a point of not looking ill. If you look ill or weak you've marked yourself out to the world as a viable target who isn't going to run as fast as the rest of the herd or flock. Hence sheep make a point of looking really fit and well until absolutely the last minute.

Now she wasn't well, and was admitting it, I could catch her and see what was up. What seems to have happened is she got an orf infection on one teat which made the teat sore, and this meant she wasn't happy at the lambs sucking that teat; this in turn meant that it wasn't sucked out and she got mastitis in it. This needn't have taken more than a couple of days to happen.

So she needed treatment and needed to come home. It was a doddle getting her into the trailer behind the quad, but catching the lambs was another matter. We couldn't catch them, they wouldn't follow and we couldn't drive them. Fortunately we managed to cut an elderly Leicester ewe and her lamb out of the rest of the flock. She was sensible and allowed herself to be driven, and her lamb and the two others stuck with her on the grounds she probably knew what was going on. So eventually we got everybody home.

And one more glimpse of how things are. You'll have doubtless seen plenty of pictures and films about lambs gambolling and frolicking. Last night about 9pm whilst it was still light I went out just to make sure one of our two remaining lambing ewes hadn't surprised us with a happy event. Out in the field behind the buildings I noticed that some of the hoggs who've lambed were also feeling the joys of spring. They too were gambolling and frolicking, with their lambs trying to keep up.

Obviously it's difficult for a lamb to run when it's trying to look stern and say, "Mum, honestly, behave!"

A sea of Maize and the full moon.

You can tell that it's spring. They're planting maize, and round here a lot of it is planted under 'plastic'.

It can be a little disconcerting, when you look across at a field from a distance because it looks in some cases as if the tide has come in a little far, it's the same colour as the sea!

So why do it? Maize needs warm ground. I remember an American telling me that he'd got some land attached to his farmhouse. He had a proper job and didn't farm as such. Not only that, but there was too little land to support a family even if he did want to farm it.

Still, he worked with a neighbouring farmer and effectively used him as a contractor. It meant that the neighbouring farmer could spread his costs across more land, and the chap who was talking to me still made some profit off his ground. (From memory, his profit was mainly in the form of pork for his freezer.)

That year he'd asked his older neighbour when they would be planting maize (or corn as it is over there). The old chap just smiled and said that they'd do it on the full moon. Well that didn't make a lot of sense to my correspondent but he reasoned that the old lad had been planting maize far longer than he had. Anyway he had to go away for a few days. When he came home the maize was planted and the moon was still not full. So he asked his neighbour what had happened.

The old chap just smiled again, and explained that the 'full moon' is when you can sit with your bare buttocks on the soil and the ground doesn't feel damp or cold.

And that's what the plastic is for. It gives each maize seedling its own little greenhouse, so you can plant maize earlier in the season. This means that you have a longer growing season which in turn means you get more crop. Admittedly it's more expensive to grow, but experience shows that the cost per ton harvested is the same, with or without plastic, but with the plastic mulch you get more tons. Given a steadily increasing population needs more food, one way or another, we need more tons.

Now what about the plastic? Well firstly it's biodegradable. Soil bacteria love these plastics and dispose of them pretty promptly. They break them down into basic ingredients. So you're left with more soil bacteria, carbon, carbon dioxide and with some plastics, nitrates. These are just the sort of things a growing plant wants to snap up and utilise.

There's a pretty good reason why we use biodegradable plastics. The Chinese have been using polyethylene sheeting across about fifty million acres. From their point of view polyethylene has serious advantages over the biodegradable plastics. It's a lot cheaper, (a quarter of the price) and because it lasts until harvest it reduces water demand by twenty to thirty percent. Also it provides a 'better greenhouse' than biodegradable plastics allowing the Chinese to not merely sow earlier, but in some cases sow land that they might not otherwise be able to sow. Unfortunately they're now suffering serious problems from polyethylene pollution in the soil. Apparently it's now got to the stage where the National People's Congress is drafting the country's first soil pollution law.

So that's why ours is biodegradable, and we're left with happy soil bacteria and plant food.

A haiku for swimming sheep

Just because somebody can do something, it doesn't mean that they should. Just as some men shouldn't wear lycra, sheep shouldn't swim. Once they've been sheared it's not such a problem. Like cattle they can swim reasonably well and have good natural buoyancy. But in spring, before they're sheared, sheep really shouldn't swim. All that sodden wet fleece just weighs them down.

But anyway I was there with quad bike, trailer and their food. I drove into the field heading for a nice dry level bit they've not been fed on previously and off to the right I heard bleating. A short detour and I could see a sheep stuck in the beck.

Now calling it a beck gives it a quaint rustic feel. You can almost see the water trickling between stones, with damsel flies hovering above. Except that in our case the beck looks more like an anti-tank ditch dug to stiffen the eastern defences of Barrow, and the bottom is clay rather than stone.

So I fed the sheep and drove back to see what our swimming sheep was doing. Well now she was on the other side of the beck. Fine, now I know where we stand I'll go home and get the full kit.

So I did. I got home and got the crook. Forget what you've ever read about crooks. This one I made myself for this very job. What happens if you don't have a crook is that you descend the steeply sloping side of the beck ready to grab the sheep and pull her out, only to have her move to the other side.

So you clamber up onto the field, walk the hundred yards to the bridge, walk the hundred yards back on the other side of the beck, clamber down the bank, and lo, the sheep moves to the opposite bank.

So my crook is twelve feet of mild steel round bar. We heated the end and it was then bent over to make it the traditional crook shape. It gives me a reach of about ten feet and it means that I get to choose which side of the beck we work from.

Then there's the rope. It's a climbing rope somebody gave us. Apparently climbers discard their ropes at a certain point because they're no longer safe to climb with. Farmers discard ropes as well. Normally when there are so many knots in it you can use it as a step ladder!

I've lost track of how many livestock this one has pulled out of water. When it's been used we just pop it into the washing machine and it's as good as new.

Finally there's me. At some point in these rescues there can come a point where you realise you cannot pull 100kg of sheep plus a further 50kg of sodden fleece uphill. You've got to go down into the beck and get your knees under her and lift her up. Given that the bottom is mud, you can easily end up waist deep in the muck.

So I put on a pair of shorts and discarded my wellies, wearing instead a pair of old trainers. These trainers are so old and disreputable that I genuinely don't care if they get lost in the mud at the bottom of the beck. Now properly equipped and ready I set off to rescue our water loving ewe.

One comment I might make at this point is that whilst it's May, it's still not the weather for riding on a quadbike wearing shorts. But setting mere personal discomfort to one side I pressed on. I arrived in the field to see her looking up in some alarm at me, the quadbike and all the assembled equipment. She'd moved further along the beck. Here the bank was perhaps more trodden down. So alarmed she was by my sudden reappearance that she managed to struggle up out of the water, flounder her way up the bank and stood dripping by the quad trailer.

Move along citizen, nothing to see here.

Stuck in deep water
Hears the quad rattling loud
With one bound, she's free

And at last.

Well it's finally happened, the last ewe has lambed. After just over two months, they've finally finished. The last ewe, (really she was a hogg as it's her first lamb) was been outside with the others rather than being kept on her own in the pens. This is because sheep don't really like being on their own.
Anyway somebody noticed her straining in the field, nipped out to check and decided the feet looked a bit big for comfort. So we fetched her in. (In reality we fetched all of them in because be damned if she was coming in on her own.) Anyway we got her into a pen on her own and with a little bit of help she has produced one rather large lamb.
In a way there's an element of symbolism here, a sign that the year is rolling on and already we're preparing for next year's lambing. Her lamb was fathered by a tup lamb who had been kept on to work as a tup.

He ran with a few of the hoggs last year just to ensure he was fertile and knew what the game was. This morning provides, I suppose, a resounding 'yes' to both questions. So he'll be on the first team for this coming autumn.
At the same time, as each batch of ewes and lambs is coming in, they're getting wormed, and whilst we're doing that, their feet are checked. A couple of ewes who have had mastitis since they lambed have been marked down to go. They've lost a quarter and if they lambed again they wouldn't have the milk to feed their lambs. Also we check teeth. When they get to a certain age, sheep start losing teeth. In the wild this would lead to them growing weaker (because they cannot eat as efficiently) and they'd soon be picked out of the flock by predators. Again, without the ability to eat properly it can be a struggle for us to carry them through the winter, they'd probably reabsorb their lambs and certainly wouldn't be able to produce enough milk to feed a lamb. So they're marked down to go.
At the same time, an eye is being cast over the ewe lambs born this year and some could be kept to grow on for breeding.

The sense of the seasons and years rolling by is enhanced by the fact that we've got another Defra consultation document on what agriculture should look like. This one has the unfortunate title of Health and Harmony. It makes it sound like one of those 1950s magazines which had photos of scantily clad young ladies going through their exercise regimes. As usual Defra trying to square the circle of wanting cheap food so that people can afford to keep the economy ticking over by buying consumer goods. At the same time they want to keep a 19th century countryside. Yet a century ago it took the average worker an hour and eighteen minutes to earn a pound of butter. Now it takes the same worker a mere ten minutes to earn the same pound of butter. The price of flour has fallen by 88% in the same period, the price of eggs by 92%.

And it's spring so we, like pretty well every other farmer, are making sure that our details are correct on the RPA computers.

Last year they had turned a pond into a salt marsh and turned another field into a watercourse. Also an electricity substation had become a farm building.

So last year we contacted them and got everything changed back to what it should be. The forms were then filled in and sent off and everything was correct.

And now my lady wife looks at the pre-populated forms and discovers that the pond has been turned back into a salt marsh, the field is once more a watercourse and the electricity substation has turned back into "An animal shelter on bare soil."

"Trust the computer, the computer is your friend!"

The question I would like answering is this. Given that their staff manually corrected things last year when we told them what had happened, does the Rural Payments Agency have software that spontaneously generates errors, or do they employ somebody whose job is merely to go round changing things at random?

Hanging on in there

There has been a story circulating in the media about a cow wearing a bra. Basically the lady in question had two rear teats which are a bit close to the ground, so her calf tends to suck the front two teats because it's easier. So the farmer put a bra over the front two teats which means the calf cannot get to them and has to suck the rear teats first. At this point it's worth taking a diversion into dairy cow breeding. When I was a child, AI in cattle was just taking off.

Now dairy farmers had always tried to breed cows who had a good grip on their udder and with hand milking, wanted a cow to have a teat of reasonable length. Also if the cow is suckled the calf wants a teat that is of a certain optimum size. Too small and it'll struggle to suck, too large it'll struggle to get the damned thing in its mouth.

AI in cattle got a boost with computerisation where you could compare all sorts of records, from all over the world. Also it became possible for bulls to have daughters on several continents. So a bull's mother, sisters, (because they share his genetics) and eventually his daughters will be assessed on udder depth, the shape and attachment of the rear udder, the length and attachment of the fore udder and the cleft between the left and right hand sides of the udder. This latter isn't a fashion statement, it's an indicator of the strength of the suspensory ligament.

Then you come to teat placement (the last thing you want is them sticking out of the sides. Not only is it disconcerting for a calf but it's a nightmare when you're trying to put a milking machine on. Then the teats themselves should be cylindrical, neither too long nor too short and neither too thick nor too thin.

As you can see, no underwear model or plastic surgeon has gone into the sort of practical detail that the average dairy farmer considers.

Now cattle generations come round quite quickly. If a cow gets in calf to a certain bull, in nine months you'll have a calf, and in two years that calf will have her first calf. So you can see the results of a breeding policy within your working lifetime.

Now when I was young, you'd get old cows walking into the parlour with 'bags like swills' and teats which stuck out at all sorts of angles. Not only that but you'd have cows with udders where they've lost control of the rear udder and it's just sagged. Thanks to fifty years of breeding you see that a lot less amongst dairy cows.

But of course, with cattle bred for beef, they've used different breeding criteria. Udder shape never really figured in their calculations because they never milked the animal.

Beef cows don't produce a lot of milk and concentrate on feeding their calf.

At this point it might be worth looking at the length of life of dairy cattle. Apparently it's about three lactations (so about five to six years.)

However this is determined by a lot of things. The animal's health, her yield, various traits and temperament, and whether she will get back in calf or not. So whilst it's not uncommon for a dairy herd to have a lot of cows aged eight to twelve and a few old stalwarts in their teens, some cows will milk for one lactation and will be sold because they're not as good as their contemporaries.

What is interesting is that fifty years ago I remember reading about this topic in a farming magazine. The writer had looked back at figures collected over fifty years previously (so this takes us back to before the First World War.) He was complaining that the average life of dairy cows had been three lactations back then and hadn't improved in his day. So in spite of intensification etc, the life span of the average dairy cow hasn't altered much in over a century.

Can you have too much garlic?

Some years ago I remember chatting to a man who worked for the now long disbanded Milk Marketing Board. One of his jobs was working as a trouble shooter for the board, helping solve those little problems that crop up.

One problem was caused by wild garlic. A dairy herd on his patch escaped out of their field one night and wandered into the local wood where they picnicked enthusiastically on wild garlic. Being dairy cows who had merely extended their grazing range slightly, next morning, at the normal time they all made their way home for milking as usual, so when the farmer went out go collect them, they were waiting at the gate as they always did.

So he milked them and the milk went into his bulk tank. As he finished milking he got a jug of milk out of the tank for the house (because cold unpasturised milk is the finest thing in the world to drink or pour over breakfast cereals.) The tanker driver came to collect the milk, sampled it and then sucked it into his tanker. At this point two unfortunate facts ought to be mentioned. The farmer has no sense of smell and the tanker driver had a severe cold, and therefore no sense of smell.

The farmer went in with the jug of milk, had his breakfast and was just going out again when his wife arrived home from the school run. Her first comment was along the lines of, 'Have you been eating garlic for breakfast?"

Of course he hadn't, but his breath smelled of it. As did the milk! Lactating mothers everywhere have to be careful what they eat because it can taint or flavour the milk. Muttering something that might have been 'oh dear' he phoned the company that collected his milk. The transport manager, when things were explained to him said, 'Oops' (or something with a similar number of letters.) He then checked to see which dairy the tanker was delivering to and phoned them. He went on to discover that the one tanker had been used to top up three storage silos at the dairy. At this point both he and the dairy manager said 'Lawks amercy' and the dairy manager phoned the chap who was telling me all this.

He went to the farm and got the farmer to put a claim in on his insurance policy. The MMB used to insist we all had that sort of cover, I think it might even have been arranged through them.

Then he went to the dairy and stood next to the manager and stared hard at the three silos.

Now in theory they could have just had it carted away and disposed of as waste because the insurance company would pay for it. But the rep from the insurance company came and joined them in the yard to survey the damage, and he suggested that perhaps something could be done to save a total loss.

So my contact remembered a small butter making plant he'd worked with in the past. He'd got them a contract to make kosher butter. They didn't do it all the time, but when asked they'd stop the plant. Then they'd clean everything absolutely spotlessly, and with a rabbi in attendance they'd make the kosher butter. Then they'd get on with making ordinary butter. They quite liked the contract. Not only did they get to do a few extra really good deep cleans each year; they got paid to do them. Anyway they took this wild garlic tainted milk and made garlic butter. Which is fair enough, so far so good. But who is going to buy a considerable quantity of butter which includes a purely arbitrary amount of garlic. My contact did try, but there were no takers, so it was sold to the Intervention Board. They paid a base price for it, thus saving the insurance company and other policy holders a reasonable amount of money. Indeed you, dear reader, might even be one of the people who benefited indirectly from it.

Several years later the Intervention Board, despairing of ever selling any of this butter, sold it to the East Germans who burned it in power stations.

Lord alone knows how that happened!

It's my experience that after a while all sorts of people get to know of your existence. Frankly sometimes it can be a damned nuisance. Over the years I've ended up talking to all sorts of people, some of whom probably were certifiable. There again at other times it can be fascinating and can open doors into an entirely different world.

But anyway, more than a couple of decades ago now, I got this phone-call completely out of the blue from a group of farming activists.

"Is Jim Webster there?"

"Speaking."

"Oh good. We wondered if you could find out who's responsible for the Royal parks in London."

"……….."
"You see we've already got a freeman of the city who'll help us drive sheep across London Bridge but we thought we could graze them in the park and talk to people about agriculture afterwards."
Think about it, why wouldn't I help them?

So I set to work. Who on earth did I know who might know the right people? Actually this is the secret. The secret is not merely knowing stuff, it's knowing people who know the people who know stuff.
So I thought of Caroline. I felt she was the best person to ask. So that evening I phoned Caroline.
She listened as I explained and immediately told me to phone George. George wouldn't know who controlled the Royal Parks, but he'd know who I ought to talk it. And I was to tell George that Caroline had told me to speak to him.
Well you don't get better than that, so I phoned George. Remember I'm phoning him right out of the blue and he almost certainly doesn't know me from Adam.
"Hi George, it's Jim Webster here and Caroline told me to talk to you."
George burst out laughing and merely commented that 'To hear is to obey.'
So I explained to George, and he laughed again and then gave me the names of two ladies who were sure to be happy to help. And of course he told me to mention that George and Caroline were supporting me.

So I phone the first lady. She picks up the phone and as I'm talking to her there is another conversation in the background. Father is shouting upstairs to see if his daughter will sweet-talk her boyfriend into driving the mower tractor tomorrow when they're silaging. The impression I got was that daughter had other plans for the day that didn't involve grass.

But anyway the lady was very helpful, thought the sheep scheme was brilliant and gave me a name and phone number for the person who organised things in the Royal parks. But she told me to phone lady number two as well. So I phoned lady number two. Half way through our conversation it got a bit chaotic because a weak lamb that had been in the warming oven of the aga had recovered enough to escape. So she continued to talk to me with phone in one hand, lamb in the other and two Border Collies watching her carefully to make sure everything sheep related was done properly. Lady Two gave me the same name and number as Lady One and we agreed it was a result.
So I phoned the group of activists and gave them the name and phone number so they could make their formal approach during office hours. Given I'd managed to get the information for them in less than five hours I thought it was pretty slick to be honest.

Anyway, it had meant I'd been on the phone talking to people for most of the evening. (Proper phones this, landlines, none of your mobile nonsense. Back then mobile phones were so big I couldn't have held one up for that length of time!)
But as I wandered through to the other end of the house my mother asked why on earth I'd been on the phone so long. So I explained to her. I even mentioned the names of Lady One and Lady Two.
She burst out laughing. Apparently these two ladies had, in their youth, been the contemporaries and disreputable friends of Princess Margaret, 'It Girls' before the term was invented.
Me, I think they turned out all right.
And no, I cannot remember if they did end up putting sheep in the Royal parks.
But isn't it great that so many apparently respectable people are perfectly happy to help with some bizarre and off the wall stunt to support the industry and way of life they love.
The anarchic streak runs deep in all the best people

It's unseasonably warm

It's sunny, it's even hot at times, and I haven't worn waterproofs for at least a fortnight.
So what are we up to? Sheep are doing OK, lambs are growing nicely. They always say that lamb has to be cooked twice, once outside in the sun and once inside in the oven. But they're looking well and bouncing happily. Otherwise we've finished first cut silage and are now waiting for the grass to grow again. At the same time in one of the ponds we have a swan who's waiting for her eggs to hatch. She's nesting on a pond we put a few trees round nearly thirty years ago. We pretty regularly get swans nesting here, and certainly geese, coots, moorhens and the occasional duck.
Actually we've seen a definite increase in the wildlife round here over the last few decades and much of it is due to the efforts of the local Wildfowlers. They will hunt ducks and geese (in season) for the table. Also in season they'll take the occasional pheasant and help keep down the number of rabbits if they start getting out of hand.
The wildfowlers help in two ways. The first is that over the years they've done work to make nesting sites better, and have even worked with farmers to produce more nesting sites. But perhaps even more importantly, they help police who does and who doesn't hunt. So whereas most farmers will be wary about crossing those who hunt with lurchers or other dogs, or shoot without permission (because they know where we live, and do you really want to come home to a barn fire?) the Wildfowlers can be straight on the phone and can turn up in court to provide witnesses if needed.
It depends on the area, but round here our wildfowlers and hunters are ordinary working class lads out of the local town, and they're great because they provide a bridge between town and country. This is because whilst they live in town, they have a genuine love of the countryside and do try to understand the rural world.

I remember talking to one, relatively early one morning. He worked month on, month off, on the rigs. So he reckoned that the thing that kept him sane was being able to come home to his family and then next day go out early in the morning; long before the rest of his family were out of bed, and just walk for two or three hours with dog and gun. Perhaps he'd provide their evening meal (because he could cook game as well as merely shoot and prepare it) or perhaps he wouldn't, but he was there with a purpose. Importantly, it was his purpose, his priorities were the priorities that really mattered and the company, the various inspectorates, the union and everybody else who made his working life so stressful could just go hang.

We see others as well. I know one chap who does not enjoy good health but took up metal detecting. When he's up to it we'll see him and he'll get a day in and he always looks better for it.

Those who want to just walk are well provided for, there's a reasonable network of paths and quiet lanes round here, but somehow we've got to provide for the others as well, those with different excuses for getting out into the countryside, but still have that same driving need to just immerse themselves.

There again, thinking about it; isn't it a really sad indictment of decades of government and local authority town planning, that the spaces they have created for people to live in are so toxic that people can only survive by getting out of them and spending time in places where the planners have never set foot?

Sheep, just because!

My lady wife had to get another car. It's not new, but it is newer. Thus every time she starts it, a disembodied female voice informs her that 'Emergency Assistance is not operational.'

It sums up so much of modern technology. This is a service we never asked for, haven't got a clue what it does, cannot use because neither of us have smart phones (why pay for a smart phone contract when it spends 99% of its life switched off because we live in an area with no signal) and what's more there appears to be no way of switching the disembodied voice off. Or at least none that our dealer can come up with.

Still it does give me the occasional chance to hear my wife mutter, "Oh shut up you idiot woman" when she's got enough on her plate without having to contemplate the ineffectuality of technological innovation.

It has to be admitted that I treat the bizarre foibles of modern technology with casual disdain. With the obvious exception of Windows 10, which has pushed back the frontiers of futility and has taken pointless innovation to new and self-destructive levels, there is little that modern technology can offer in the way of incomprehensible behaviour that even a perfectly ordinary sheep couldn't match.

Because we're in May, and Furness does May really well, we've cut back the feed we're giving to the ewes. Because they're busy producing milk for lambs, the ewes need plenty of energy and in March and April this isn't available from the grass. But as one old farming saying has it, "You can milk bullocks in May." The grass is perfect for milk production, there is plenty of it and not only that but the lambs are old enough to be eating a fair bit of grass themselves.

So rather than me turn up with quad, trailer, Sal, and several buckets of feed, the ewes just get Sal and me. Unless that is, I'm in a rush to be somewhere and then they get a quad, Sal and me.

If it's just Sal and me the ewes glare at me, some even wandering across to check up on the off chance I might just produce something for them, conjuring it up out of thin air.
But if the quad appears, the entire flock concentrates on us and when we turn to leave the field they stream after us like some ovine version of the Keystone Cops.
The propensity to associate the quad with food is immediately dispelled if you blow the horn. To the sheep (and through observation, to Sal) once the horn is blown the game changes. The quad morphs instantaneously from potential feed dispenser into the rounder up of laggards.

Whilst we're on about sheep surprising you, it might be worth mentioning the five hoggs in the church yard. They're keeping the grass down. The problem is it would cost an awful lot of money to pay somebody to mow it. Anybody volunteering to do it would find themselves spending days at a time wielding the strimmer because there are too many curbs and suchlike to allow proper mowing with a lawn mower. So the answer is sheep. (Actually to get 'sheep' as an answer, you've got to be looking at a very specialist subset of questions.)
From a pure grazing/grassland management point of view we really put the sheep in too late, but then we don't want to spoil the rather spectacular display of daffodils. So the sheep spend summer playing catch up.
Now this year there are five hoggs in the church yard. They ran with the tup last backend but being young it's always touch and go whether they'll end up in lamb, and so when the last ewe lambed on May 8th we weren't surprised that these young ladies were obviously not going to lamb.
So next year is obviously going to be their big year, and they were kept to grow on with the idea that they'd come into the flock as shearlings. So this morning I turned up at the church to check on the five to see four running towards me, and I wondered where the fifth was.
She was following; looking over her shoulder to make sure that her lamb was keeping up with her.

Isn't the air thick down here?

Every silver lining has a cloud. Living here, every so often you get Herdwicks. Herdwick Hoggs are brought down from the fells to overwinter, and some of them wander off. They wander off because they're Herdwicks. It's just what they do. "I wander therefore I am."
Anyway one of them wandered during the course of this winter and ended up with us. Picture her, all brown with a white face. The rest of the flock are decent, respectable breeds. Even as I stop to look at them, they're starting to form something which looks like the start of a defensive circle because Sal (at the back) is starting to gather them up.
Defensive circles work well with Musk ox but somehow sheep don't have what it takes. So seconds later, in deference to Sal's efforts, the sheep were moving in approximately the right direction.
But anyway, we are temporary custodian of a Herdwick. At some point an owner might turn up, who knows. But this process of wintering young breeding female sheep in the lowlands is very old. It's been done for centuries.
But it's not without issues. The bureaucratic complexities of the process are worth exploring.
Generally I'd say most of the environmental agencies are in favour of overwintering sheep off the fells. Depending on the fell and the environmental scheme, they will even make a financial contribution towards the process. It is, from their point of view as an arm of government, "A good thing," and one the state, in some cases, supports financially for environmental reasons.
But then you come to another arm of the State, Animal Health. Livestock wandering about all willy-nilly is frowned upon. 'You don't know what they've got!' For epidemiological reasons the state vets would cut down the number of animal movements to the absolute minimum.
So you get animal movement systems set up so that every movement is tracked, by a farmer who reads the ear-tag and sends the details to the appropriate authority. This is an EU idea by the way.

Then you get a supermarket that comes along and decides that it can make something out of this. To try and entice you the consumer into paying more for 'higher welfare' the supermarket announces that it will not buy animals that have been on more than 'x' farms (where 'x' is a number chosen in a pretty arbitrary manner by the marketing people).

So an ancient system that is approved of by one arm of the state and closely monitored by another arm of the state is being discriminated against by a retailer who thinks they might get a couple of cheap brownie points out of it for their marketing department.

But the more we look at it the more complicated it gets. The EU pronounced that sheep would have an electronic tag so each was an individual traceable under all circumstances.

Now set aside the possible existential angst a sheep might experience on discovering that it is officially an individual. The idea was that the farmer would wave a stick reader at the sheep and it would tell him the ID of the sheep.

The farmer then submits to the local trading standards department a list of the individual IDs of the sheep that he or she is moving.

Obviously this should be done electronically, one database chittering away in machine-code to another. Except that government might legislate for a system but couldn't afford to actually put it in place. So when the farmer sends information to trading standards (on paper) to say these 57 individual animals (with all their details) have moved. Trading standards immediately ignore the individual animals and write down 57 sheep moved off that farm to the auction.

So government introduced a system that the industry didn't particularly want and government cannot afford to run anyway.

Foxes, Sal, cultural dissonance and virtually the whole tree!

Have you ever wondered whether you were breaking the law or not? This morning I was quietly minding my own business, walking round the farm checking to see that various batches of sheep were OK. Of course I had Sal with me because even when there's no formal work to be done, she can still be useful. She'll find the ones who're snoozing quietly in obscure corners and get them running back to the others. A sheep who runs back to the others is generally a healthy sheep. A sheep who just stares blankly at Sal and ignores her is, in all probability, ill.

Anyway this morning I was walking across one field and Sal set off into a big patch of rushes and long grass. Unfortunately she's not a tall dog and just disappeared into them. Every so often she'd spring vertically using all four feet in an attempt to spot her way out.

Then suddenly I saw a fox leaving the rushes at speed. This was followed by Sal, also moving at speed. The fox accelerated and made a run for the beck. In Sal's mind, this is the equivalent of a felon making a run for the state line. So of course she accelerated as well. Anyway the fox swam the beck and ran up the other side and away. Sal stopped on our side of the beck leaving me pondering whether I had been hunting?

After all "A person will be deemed to be hunting if s/he engages or participates in the pursuit of a wild mammal and one or more dogs are employed in that pursuit."

Now I would put forward as my defence that I didn't actually participate. Frankly there's no way I could keep up with either Sal or the fox. Indeed I didn't even shout encouragement from the side-lines.

Not only that but I would have suggested to my learned friend that a Border Collie bitch who takes it upon herself to remove a fox from amongst her sheep isn't hunting. She's merely doing her job.

Still we shall leave that vexed legal issue behind us and continue with our perambulations, checking sheep.

Then as I left one field I discovered somebody had dumped a lot of chopped up lengths of Leylandii in the gateway. So after I'd been to church, Sal and I returned with the quad and trailer to collect them.

Now here's where the cultural dissonance comes in. Somebody is proudly tidying their garden etc, and what do they do with their rubbish? Put it in the car and drive out into the countryside to dump it! The tip is probably nearer. So they're sitting proudly in their garden, basking in the praise of everybody who's saying, "You've got this looking nice." When actually they're just some muppet who dumps their rubbish in gateways.

But actually it gets even more confusing because frankly, if the person had come into our yard with it, I'd have helped them unload the car onto our log pile. It can stay there, dry out a bit and then I'll cut it up and it'll help keep our house warm this winter. To some rubbish dumping muppet who lives in a house with central heating, it's garbage to be dumped. For those of us rural dwellers for whom affordable gas central heating is an impossible dream, it's a resource. We recycle stuff like that for its energy content.

I suppose it's probably summer

Whilst we've had a lot of hot dry weather up here, the ground was so wet that we've seen very little sign of grass burning off. Indeed everything still looked pretty green even before the last lot of rain. This is especially true of anything deep rooted.

We aren't a big farm but we have an interesting collection of soil types. Down on our bottom land we're right on the clay, and in hot weather it cracks nicely. We really need a dry spell at some point in the year to crack the clay. It lets the air in and also improves the drainage. Indeed if it is well cracked, when it rains, the ground holds the water rather than having it just run off the surface and into the beck.

There are other signs that we've moved firmly from spring to summer. Even a quick glance at this field of barley will show that it's starting to 'turn.' From now on it's going to stop growing and start ripening. I suspect further south the combines will be working in a month.

One thing I've stopped doing is feeding sheep. The lambs are old enough to be able to get their nutrition out of grass. At the same time the ewes will be slowly cutting down the amount of milk they produce so they too can manage entirely on the grass they eat.

Now Sal and I walk round sheep, and their reaction to me is different. Whereas when I was on the quad they'd mob me looking for concentrates, now when I walk in they might drift across just to check. But all in all they're starting to lose interest and a lot of them would rather sit in the shade and just watch me go past.

Still, it has to be said that on a fine morning, looking sheep isn't a bad job. I worked out it took me about an hour and that means I must be walking nearly three miles.

Luckily my co-worker, who is faster than me, is happy enough to wait for me to catch up.

The world of cute lambs and the tuna melt panini.

It has been said that the world is a magical place full of people waiting to be offended by something. This is probably true, but today, perhaps by accident, I might not offend anybody at all. I know it seems unlikely but in an infinite universe pretty well anything should be possible.

So this morning another hogg lambed. Working backwards on our fingers she wasn't technically anyway near any of the tups when the lamb was conceived.

So how had she managed it? All I can say is that she isn't the first young lady who has wandered in shyly carrying a baby and hoping against hope that the overall atmosphere of cuteness will stop people asking difficult and embarrassing questions. So anyway the proud mum has brought her offspring into a parched world which is somewhat at odds with the world the other lambs arrived into. Instead of the 'beast from the east' we're reliving the spirit of 1976, and the only green thing in the photograph is a thistle.

When it gets old enough to discuss things with other lambs, their tales of cold winds and driving rain are going to be met with stubborn disbelief. And of course, when you're this age, grass has always been brown and crispy.

Still it's happy and Mum's happy and everything's fine.

Sal is also happy. Sal is a small Border Collie bitch with a taste for the finer things in life. We already knew she had a liking for pizza and warm sausage rolls. But the other day, through circumstances too complicated to discuss now, we acquired a very slightly time expired tuna melt panini.

Now I realise that the world contains many people who adore tuna. I admit to being someone who doesn't particularly like tuna. So I sliced it as you would a loaf and dropped some pieces in the bottom of Sal's food bowl before adding the biscuits.

Sal has added tuna melt panini to her list of foods that make for a superior dining experience.

So not long after feeding her I noticed that most of the sheep had moved from one field to the next. This is a good thing, tomorrow they'll have to be fastened in the other field anyway so that we can take a fence down. So I collected Sal with the idea of moving the rest of them through and shutting the gate on them.

Sal shot off towards the sheep, screeched to a halt and ran back to her food bowl, grabbed another piece of her panini and then went to move the sheep. Personally I suspect that it's the cheese rather than the tuna but even so, she seems to enjoy it. I can imagine the advertising slogan. 'Border collies prefer our panini to sheep.'

Now amongst the sheep were our young Mum and her lamb. They'd found a place in the shade, sitting in a cattle creep feeder. Sal rapidly moved the rest of the sheep through the gate and then came back to glare at the laggard. Time was wasting; panini doesn't eat itself you know.

But the concerned Mum wasn't going out of her way to be cooperative. Sal slots nicely into the 'wolf' end of a sheep's recognition chart and there was no way she was taking her darling child out there into the blazing sun with wolves prowling.

Sal couldn't get in because our young mum nicely blocked the entrance and was perfectly happy to come out at speed, forehead first if Sal tried it on. So eventually I had to go in, collect the lamb and mum followed behind me, muttering under her breath about the fact that the world seems to be going to the dogs.

Sal trotted behind, moderately happy with the way things were finally moving forward.

Then with the last two in the field and the gate shut, she glanced briefly at me before running off to finish her tea.

Printed in Great Britain
by Amazon